Classic Steelers

CLASSIC SPORTS

Jonathan Knight, Series Editor

Classic Bucs: The 50 Greatest Games in Pittsburgh Pirates History
    David Finoli

Classic Steelers: The 50 Greatest Games in Pittsburgh Steelers History
    David Finoli

Classic Steelers

THE 50 GREATEST GAMES IN
PITTSBURGH STEELERS HISTORY

David Finoli

Black Squirrel Books™

An imprint of The Kent State University Press
Kent, Ohio 44242   www.KentStateUniversityPress.com

BLACK SQUIRREL BOOKS™ 🐿™

Frisky, industrious black squirrels are a familiar sight on the Kent State University campus and the inspiration for Black Squirrel Books™, a trade imprint of The Kent State University Press. www.KentStateUniversityPress.com.

Library of Congress Catalog Card Number 2012048458
ISBN 978-1-60635-198-7
Manufactured in the United States of America

Library of Congress Cataloging-in-Publication Data
Finoli, David, 1961–
  Classic Steelers : the 50 greatest games in Pittsburgh Steelers history / David Finoli.
     pages. cm.
Includes bibliographical references.
ISBN 978-1-60635-198-7 (pbk.) ∞
1. Pittsburgh Steelers (Football team)—History. I. Title.
  GV956.P57F56 2014
  796.332'640974886—dc23
                                2013042595

18 17 16 15 14   5 4 3 2 1

To my own personal Steeler Nation: Viv, Matt, Cara, Tony, Ma Pansino, Nancy, Fletch, Bill, and Tom, with whom I've enjoyed the joys and pitfalls of our favorite team for the past five decades.

Contents

Acknowledgments

Many people were instrumental in the completion of this book. To start, there is my incredible, supportive family that makes my life a true joy: Viv, my wife of 28 years, and my three children, Tony, Matt, and Cara.

My extended family has also been there through the highs and lows of my life over the years. My parents, Domenic and Eleanor, my brother Jamie, his wife, Cindy, and his daughters, Marissa and Brianna, my sister Mary and her husband, Matthew, and all my loving aunts, uncles, and cousins, as well as Vivian Pansino and her daughter, Nancy, who have been going to Steelers games with my wife and me to cheer them on since 1985.

A big thank-you also has to go Joyce Harrison of the Kent State University Press, my copy editor Rebekah Cotton, and Jonathan Knight, the editor of the "Classic Sports" series, who made putting this book together a wonderful experience.

Additionally, I must recognize the helpful people in the microfilm department at the Carnegie Library in Pittsburgh who have been there to point me in the right direction when I'm stuck.

Finally, I offer a huge thank-you to my partners in crime: Bill Ranier, Tom Aikens, and Chris Fletcher, who not only helped out when needed with these projects but who also relived the trials and tribulation of the Steelers with me since before the glory days.

Introduction

On November 29, 1970, a nine-year-old boy entered brand-new Three Rivers Stadium to see his first Pittsburgh Steelers game. Their opponent, as explained to him by his father, a longtime Steelers fan, was the team's bitter rivals, the Cleveland Browns. As the Steelers dismantled the Browns 28–9 that afternoon, the boy noticed that a group of Pittsburgh fans sitting nearby had grabbed a Cleveland pennant from a distraught Browns fan and set it on fire. While a little disturbed by the celebratory act, the boy developed an instant understanding of the rivalry, and a love affair with the Steelers was born.

That young boy was me, and the victory inspired a love of Steelers football, one that was strengthened even further two years later when I had the opportunity to see the Steelers' first postseason game in 25 years when they took on John Madden's Oakland Raiders. It was that day I learned two important lessons. The first was to never give up on this team, exemplified by its battling back to win on Franco Harris's miraculous "Immaculate Reception" that won the game. The second lesson came from my father's hatred of sitting in traffic. Since we were standing on the ramp on Gate C of Three Rivers as he hustled us out of the stadium to avoid the inevitable traffic jam that would follow when the greatest play in NFL History occurred, I learned to never leave a close game before the clock hit zero.

From that point on, for both me and the generations of fans that have followed, Steelers football has been nothing short of legendary: eight Super Bowl appearances, a league-record six Lombardi Trophies, and fifteen trips to the AFC championship game. The Pittsburgh Steelers are among the most successful franchises in the NFL over the last five decades. Wildly popular, there are over 700 "Steelers Bars" across the nation and in opposing stadiums in which the Steelers play; black-and-gold shirts often outnumber those of the hometown team.

But it wasn't always that way. Before that special 1972 season, the franchise was among the biggest jokes in the league. Founded in 1933, in their first 39 seasons, the Steelers had played exactly one postseason game of substance, a

21–0 loss to the Philadelphia Eagles for the 1947 Eastern Division crown. In fact, in those first 39 seasons, they only had eight winning records—the same number of Super Bowl appearances they would achieve over their next 39.

Through the two disparate eras there were many spectacular contests (though, of course, the vast majority came after 1972) that made picking the list of the top fifty Steelers games both difficult and a joy, reliving all those special moments.

Hopefully they will spark the same joyful memories in the Steelers aficionados who read these pages.

PIRATES 14, CHICAGO CARDINALS 13
SEPTEMBER 27, 1933

From Humble Beginnings

There's a stark difference between the National Football League of the twenty-first century and that of its humble beginnings in 1920. In its infancy, major markets such as Chicago and New York gave way to those in Decatur, Canton, Kenosha, and Muncie. As the league fought to find its footing, most teams struggled to make payroll, some folded, and most played in front of sparse crowds.

Thirteen years after the league's inception, the NFL was a more stable entity, yet it still wasn't close to the financial success of Major League Baseball or even college football. Still, the league was branching into larger markets, two of which joined in 1933 when it seemed apparent that state voters would ease the "blue law" restrictions, allowing sporting events to be played on Sundays. This permitted the NFL to add a team in Philadelphia and another in the state's second-largest city. The latter came into being when a 32-year-old former boxer and baseball player named Art Rooney, who also happened to be very adept at betting on horse racing, used the $2,500 he had made at the track on an especially good day to buy a team for the city of Pittsburgh.

A successful semi-pro baseball player, Rooney named his club after the city's Major League Baseball team, the Pirates. He then went about acquiring talent, signing players such as Tony Holm, a 25-year-old running back from Alabama who had already spent three seasons in the NFL, and the team's elder statesman—a balding hometown halfback/kicker named Mose Kelsch—who would turn out to be the hero of the franchise's first victory.

Rooney's team began to play that fall, losing to the New York Giants 23–2 in the season opener at Forbes Field, then hosted the Chicago Cardinals on a rainy Wednesday afternoon. While the blue laws were expected to allow sports to be played on Sundays, it wouldn't be official until the November elections when the citizens of Pennsylvania voted for the change. This necessitated the Steelers play their first four home games on Wednesday afternoons.

The Cardinals jumped to an early lead when defensive lineman Jim McNally picked off a lateral from Holm and rumbled 55 yards for a touchdown. Chicago's star running back Joe Lillard, the last African American to play in the NFL between 1933 and 1946, missed the point after to keep the score 6–0, but he made up for it in the second quarter by completing a touchdown pass to Hal Moe and then adding the extra point to increase the Cardinals' lead to 13–0.

For a Pirates team that would only score 67 points in the entire season, a 13-point deficit seemed insurmountable, but as more than 6,000 excited fans at Forbes Field watched, the Pirates slowly fought back

With Chicago driving down the field for another score moments later, the Pirates' Marty Kottler, a local player from Carnegie, picked off a pass and returned the interception 96 yards for the first touchdown in the history of the franchise. On to the field came 38-year-old Kelsch, with his leather helmet off, who split the uprights on the extra point to make it 13–7.

The scoring halted after that as the Cardinals, who had maintained their six-point lead, marched into Pittsburgh territory with time running out in the game. Just when it seemed like the Pirates would drop to 0–2, Chicago's Mike Koken fumbled the ball at the Pittsburgh 18. The Pirates' defense pounced on the loose ball, giving the home team one last chance.

The Pirates' James Peter "Bill" Tanguay would complete only five passes in 1933—the only season in his NFL career—but two of them would come in the next two plays and would spark the franchise's first victory. First, Tanguay hit Paul Moss for 14 yards. Then, after an illegal-substitution penalty, he once again tried to connect with Moss. The pass flew high above the goalposts (which in 1933 were in front of the end zone), but Moss leapt into the air in the back of the end zone, snagging the ball for the game-tying touchdown.

Once again, Kelsch trotted onto the field, this time with a chance to give the Pirates their first-ever lead. As he left the bench, his excited teammates patted him on the back, imploring him to "make that kick good." Kelsch did just that, putting Pittsburgh up by a point with time about to expire.[1]

The Pirates' defense held, and the game ended with the thrilled fans at Forbes Field cheering wildly for their new team as it emerged with its first win.

The victory over the Cardinals proved to be the high point of their first season as the Pirates struggled to a 3–6–2 mark. Incredibly, this win, coupled with a win two weeks later, also marked the only time the franchise would have an all-time winning percentage of .500 or better until it finally pulled over the mark once again in 2002.

Along the way, there would be more exciting wins, but it all began with this thrilling comeback on a rainy afternoon.

BOXSCORE

TEAM	1ST	2ND	3RD	4TH	FINAL
Chicago	6	7	0	0	13
Pittsburgh	0	7	0	7	14

TEAM	PLAY	SCORE
Chicago	McNally 55-yard interception return (kick no good)	6–0
Chicago	Moe pass from Lillard (Lillard kick)	13–0
Pittsburgh	Kottler 96-yard interception return (Kelsch kick)	13–7
Pittsburgh	Moss 11-yard pass from Tanguay (Kelsch kick)	13–14

STEELERS 28, CLEVELAND BROWNS 9
NOVEMBER 29, 1970

The First Glimpse

It had been a little over 12 months since the Steelers began their latest reconstruction project, and while they had improved since their 1–13 debacle in 1969, they had yet to capture the marquee victory that would show they were headed toward the championship level of football that had eluded the club since its inception in 1933.

In 1969, the Steelers had hired Chuck Noll to run the team on the field. Coinciding with Noll's arrival, the team had collected a pack of young but talented players such as Joe Greene, Terry Bradshaw, and Mel Blount. Better days were on the way—but first they needed a hallmark victory to start the ball rolling.

They had won four of their first 10 games in 1970 when their rivals, the Cleveland Browns, came to Pittsburgh for their first encounter in the Steelers' new facility, Three Rivers Stadium. To call the series a "rivalry" at this point might have been a bit of an overstatement. After defeating Pittsburgh earlier in the season in Cleveland, the Browns held a 32–9 advantage in the series and had won 11 of the previous 12 meetings. With the Steelers getting blown out by Kansas City and Cincinnati in the previous two contests leading up to this game, there was no reason to expect this encounter would be any different, despite the fact the Browns' 5–5 record was only marginally better than Pittsburgh's.

Though Bradshaw had been the first pick in the 1970 collegiate draft, he had yet to establish himself as the clear-cut starter at quarterback, and Noll went with former Notre Dame star Terry Hanratty. The decision looked brilliant as Hanratty quickly led the Steelers on an 88-yard drive to open the contest, completing an eight-yard scoring pass to receiver Ron Shanklin to put Pittsburgh ahead.

Back-to-back field goals by the Browns cut the margin to 7–6, then Hanratty suffered a blow to the head and was pulled midway in the second quarter after completing six of eight passes for 69 yards. Enter the future of the Steelers, Terry Bradshaw. But before the man they called the "Blonde Bomber" would have his first significant moment in a Pittsburgh uniform, the Steelers' defense—which had also showed previews of things to come on this afternoon—rose to the occasion with time running out in the first half.

Linebacker Chuck Allen deflected a pass from Cleveland quarterback Bill Nelsen—a former Steeler—and into the arms of safety Chuck Beatty, who returned it 30 yards for a touchdown to extend the Pittsburgh lead to 14–6.

After the Browns cut the margin to five points with a field goal set up by a Pittsburgh fumble early in the third quarter, Bradshaw put his legendary arm-strength on display. From the Pittsburgh 19, Shanklin, the Steelers' main receiver before the arrival of Lynn Swann and John Stallworth, flew down the sideline, sailing behind the Browns' secondary, and Bradshaw hit him with a long pass. The speedy receiver stayed out of the reach of Cleveland's Erich Barnes and Mike Howell to score his second touchdown of the game to make it 21–9.

The 81-yard bomb was a play that almost didn't happen. "I had something else in mind," Bradshaw admitted to reporters after the game. "But I decided to go for the long one and Shanklin was there to grab it. When this play works it's great, isn't it?"[1] Bradshaw and Co. came up with another great play in the fourth quarter, when the Steelers put an exclamation point on this signature victory. John "Frenchy" Fuqua made up for a previous fumble by taking a short screen pass at the Pittsburgh 43 and slicing through the Browns' defense for a 57-yard touchdown and the final touch to a 28–9 victory.

Even though the offense enjoyed a stellar day, piling up 425 yards, it was the emergence of what would become the vaunted "Steel Curtain" defense that really made an impact. Led by Greene and fellow youngster L. C. Greenwood, the Pittsburgh defensive line held one of the best running backs in the league, Leroy Kelly, to no yards on 10 carries. For the game, Cleveland's offense managed only 42 rushing yards and a mere 171 total.

Despite the fact the victory only improved the Steelers' record to 5–6, they pulled into a three-way tie atop the new AFC Central Division with Cleveland and Cincinnati with just three games remaining. Though they would lose each of those final contests, this victory over the Browns provided the first glimpse of what was coming. The young players who led the Steelers to triumph over Cleveland that November afternoon were the ones who would lead them out of the cellar to their eventual role as one of the dominant teams in the NFL.

BOXSCORE

TEAM	1st	2nd	3rd	4th	FINAL
Cleveland	3	3	3	0	9
Pittsburgh	7	7	7	7	28

TEAM	PLAY	SCORE
Pittsburgh	Shanklin 8-yard pass from Hanratty (Watson kick)	0–7
Cleveland	Cockroft 16-yard field goal	3–7
Cleveland	Cockroft 38-yard field goal	6–7
Pittsburgh	Beatty 30-yard interception return (Watson kick)	6–14
Cleveland	Cockroft 46-yard field goal	9–14
Pittsburgh	Shanklin 81-yard pass from Bradshaw (Watson kick)	9–21
Pittsburgh	Fuqua 57-yard pass from Bradshaw (Watson kick)	9–28

RUSHING

PITT	ATT	YDS	AVE	TD
Pearson	14	61	4.4	0
Bradshaw	5	49	9.8	0
Fuqua	12	33	2.8	0
Hoak	4	14	3.5	0
Smith	1	6	6.0	0
Wilburn	2	5	2.5	0

CLEVE	ATT	YDS	AVE	TD
Scott	10	34	3.4	0
Phipps	2	8	4.0	0
Kelly	10	0	0.0	0
Nelson	1	0	0.0	0

RECEIVING

PITT	REC	YDS	AVE	TD
Fuqua	4	116	29.0	1
Shanklin	3	121	40.3	2
Wilburn	2	29	14.5	0
Smith	1	0	0.0	0

CLEVE	REC	YDS	AVE	TD
Scott	5	32	6.4	0
Hooker	4	50	12.5	0
Kelly	3	16	5.3	0
Morin	2	39	19.5	0
H. Jones	1	20	20.0	0

PASSING

PITT	COMP	ATT	PCT	YDS	TD	INT
Hanratty	6	8	75.0	69	1	0
Bradshaw	4	9	44.4	197	2	0

CLEVE	COMP	ATT	PCT	YDS	TD	INT
Nelson	11	29	37.9	85	0	1
Phipps	4	10	40.0	72	0	0

STEELERS 21, HOUSTON OILERS 0
DECEMBER 11, 1976

The Steel Curtain

Charles Dickens's opening line of *A Tale of Two Cities*—"It was the best of times, it was the worst of times"—also categorized the 1976 Pittsburgh Steelers. To be more accurate, though, the statement should be reversed, since the Steelers' "worst of times" occurred in the first five weeks of the '76 season.

Pittsburgh was coming off back-to-back Super Bowl championships and was looking to become the first NFL team to win three in a row. Thoughts of making history soon changed to wondering if they even were going to make the playoffs after they blew a two-touchdown lead to lose the opener at Oakland and then followed it by losing three of their next four contests. In the process, starting quarterback Terry Bradshaw was injured, and, even worse, their once-dominant defense was falling apart, giving up 110 points in the five contests—nearly unthinkable over the previous two seasons. Appropriately, though, the defense would lead the turnaround, allowing only 28 points over the next eight games, including an incredible string of three consecutive shutouts. The Steelers won all eight games to salvage the season and carry them into the finale against the Houston Oilers tied for first in the AFC Central with Cincinnati and Cleveland.

For this important contest, Chuck Noll decided to start Bradshaw for the first time in six weeks, but most eyes would be on another member of the offense. Running back Rocky Bleier was 71 yards short of 1,000 rushing yards for the season, a plateau teammate Franco Harris had passed the week before. If Bleier could also hit four digits, he and Harris would become just the second pair of teammates in NFL history to accomplish the feat in the same season, joining Miami's Mercury Morris and Larry Csonka four years earlier.

Even though they had much to play for, the Steelers sputtered out of the starting gate, and the game remained scoreless through much of the first half. Noll was extremely concerned with the rustiness of his veteran quarterback and ordered his rookie backup, Mike Kruczek, to start warming up. Moments later, Houston quarterback Dan Pastorini, who was faring no better than Bradshaw, tossed an interception into the hands of Pittsburgh defensive back Mel Blount, who took the ball to the Houston 13. Noll decided to give Bradshaw one last chance and, after a couple offensive penalties, his decision paid off when Bradshaw tossed a 21-yard pass to a leaping Lynn Swann to give the Steelers a 7–0 lead. With the defense continuing its historic run of excellence, it was all the offense Pittsburgh would need.

The second half would see Bradshaw continue to struggle, but the Steelers' powerful running game would shift into gear. Bleier, who had only mustered 12 yards in the first half, was impressive in the second, finishing with 107 yards and 1,036 for the season. The popular running back was ecstatic after the game. "I'm very happy," he said. "A lot of people were pulling for it to happen."[1]

His counterpart Harris rambled for another 104 yards, including an 11-yard scoring romp in the third quarter, led by a devastating block by Bradshaw, to put the Steelers up 14–0. The offensive line, which was not at full strength due to injury, was still surprisingly effective, helping the Steelers roll up 258 yards on the ground. Fittingly, the line paved the way for Bradshaw to put the icing on the cake when he rolled into the end zone for a one-yard score to make it 21–0.

As good as the running game was though, it was the defense that put an exclamation point on the Steelers' dramatic turnaround with its fifth shutout in the final nine games. "Our defense is dangerous as hell," Noll said after the contest. "I can't say enough about our defense."[2]

It is the defense that made 1976 worth remembering for the Steelers and their fans, as the Steel Curtain raised its reputation from one of the best units in football at the time to one of the best ever to play the game.

BOXSCORE

TEAM	1st	2nd	3rd	4th	FINAL
Pittsburgh	0	7	7	7	21
Houston	0	0	0	0	0

TEAM	PLAY	SCORE
Pittsburgh	Swann 21-yard pass from Bradshaw (Gerela kick)	7–0
Pittsburgh	Harris 11-yard run (Gerela kick)	14–0
Pittsburgh	Bradshaw 1-yard run (Gerela kick)	21–0

RUSHING

PITT	ATT	YDS	AVE	TD
Bleier	22	107	4.9	0
Harris	23	104	4.5	1
Bradshaw	4	35	8.8	1
Fuqua	2	9	4.5	0
Harrison	2	3	1.5	0

HOU	ATT	YDS	AVE	TD
Willis	11	49	4.5	0
Coleman	14	49	3.5	0
Johnson	1	-5	-5.0	0

RECEIVING

PITT	REC	YDS	AVE	TD
Bleier	2	28	14.0	0
Harris	2	12	6.0	0
Swann	2	24	17.0	1
Brown	1	4	4.0	0
Stallworth	1	-2	-2.0	0

RECEIVING

HOU	REC	YDS	AVE	TD
Burrough	3	44	14.7	0
Johnson	3	19	6.3	0
Sawyer	2	13	6.5	0
Coleman	2	-5	-2.5	0
Willis	1	7	7.0	0
Alston	1	9	9.0	0
Taylor	1	8	8.0	0

PASSING

PITT	COMP	ATT	PCT	YDS	TD	INT
Bradshaw	8	19	42.1	76	1	1

HOU	COMP	ATT	PCT	YDS	TD	INT
Pastorini	13	29	44.8	95	0	1

STEELERS 29, CLEVELAND BROWNS 9
JANUARY 7, 1995

Three Out of Three Ain't Bad

Beating a division rival three times in one season isn't impossible, but history has proven it certainly isn't easy, requiring a regular season series sweep and a playoff victory over the same opponent. Since the National Football League and the American Football League merged in 1970, it's only happened 12 times. In 1995, the Steelers had an opportunity to accomplish the feat when they faced their bitter rivals, the Cleveland Browns, in a playoff game for the first time ever.

The Browns had fashioned an 11–5 record, good enough for second place in the AFC Central, a game behind the Steelers. The two games the rivals played in the regular season were both relatively close, but each time Pittsburgh was able to pull out a victory: 17–10 in Cleveland in Week 2 and then 17–7 in Pittsburgh at Three Rivers in Week 16 to clinch the division and complete the Steelers' first series sweep of the Browns in 14 years.

Cleveland was still able to secure a wild-card spot and defeated New England in the opening round of the playoffs to set up the climactic third game in Pittsburgh against the Steelers.

Both teams knew the key to the third meeting would be Cleveland quarterback Vinny Testaverde, who'd often been confused by the Steelers' defensive fronts in the previous two meetings and threw a total of six interceptions. Even if Testaverde could right the ship, to win this game, Cleveland would have to contain Pittsburgh's powerful running game. Led by Barry Foster and Bam Morris, the Steelers led the NFL with 2,180 rushing yards and had enjoyed modest success against a Cleveland defense that allowed a league-low 204 points for the season. As it turned out, both Testaverde and the Pittsburgh running game would be the difference in the game. Just not the way the Browns had hoped.

The tone was set early. Two dropped passes halted a promising Browns' drive on their first possession. Then the Steelers took command, scoring the first three times they had the ball. Kicker Gary Anderson started the proceedings by capping a 13-play, 65-yard drive with a 39-yard field goal to put Pittsburgh up 3–0. Six minutes later they made it 10–0 on a short scoring pass from quarterback Neil O'Donnell to tight end Eric Green, and shortly after that, unheralded running back John L. Williams broke free from 26 yards out to increase the Steelers lead to 17–0.

The Browns cut into the Pittsburgh advantage with a field goal, but late in the first half, the strategy concocted by Pittsburgh defensive coordinator Dom Capers made Testaverde look silly once again. The Cleveland quarterback tossed a pass into the waiting hands of Steelers' defensive back Tim McKyer with 46 seconds left, and McKyer returned it to the Browns' six-yard line. Thirty seconds later, O'Donnell put the nail in the coffin of the Brown's Super Bowl hopes with a nine-yard touchdown toss to wideout Yancey Thigpen to make the halftime score 24–3.

The onslaught continued in the second half as the Steelers tacked on a field goal after another long drive and then turned the game over to their bruising running attack to run out the clock as Barry Foster wound up with 133 yards for the afternoon. Fittingly, the Steelers' defense scored the game's final points when blitzing safety Carnell Lake sacked Testaverde in the end zone for a safety to make the final 29–9 and send Pittsburgh to the AFC Championship Game.

The Steelers' domination was reflected in nearly every statistical category. They held the ball for more than 42 minutes of the contest and outgained the Browns 424 yards to 186. Pittsburgh's defense continued its mastery over the Cleveland quarterback as Testaverde tossed two more interceptions, giving him eight for the season against the black and gold.

While the following week Pittsburgh was the victim of one of the biggest playoff upsets in NFL history, on this January Sunday they made history of their own, making it three out of three against their longtime rivals.

BOXSCORE

TEAM	1st	2nd	3rd	4th	FINAL
Cleveland	0	3	0	6	9
Pittsburgh	3	21	3	2	29

TEAM	PLAY	SCORE
Pittsburgh	Anderson 39-yard field goal	0–3
Pittsburgh	Green 2-yard pass from O'Donnell (Anderson kick)	0–10
Pittsburgh	Williams 26-yard run (Anderson kick)	0–17
Cleveland	Stover 22-yard field goal	3–17
Pittsburgh	Thigpen 9-yard pass from O'Donnell (Anderson kick)	3–24
Pittsburgh	Anderson 40-yard field goal	3–27
Cleveland	McCardell 20-yard pass from Testaverde (pass failed)	9–27
Pittsburgh	Safety, Testaverde tacked by Lake in the end zone	9–29

RUSHING

PITT	ATT	YDS	AVE	TD
Foster	24	133	5.5	0
Morris	22	60	2.7	0
Williams	2	43	21.5	1
Tomczak	3	2	0.7	0

CLEVE	ATT	YDS	AVE	TD
Byner	9	43	4.8	0
Hoard	3	8	2.7	0
Metcalf	5	4	0.8	0

RECEIVING

PITT	REC	YDS	AVE	TD
Mills	5	117	23.4	0
Williams	4	20	5.0	0
Green	3	21	7.0	1
Hastings	2	18	9.0	0
Thigpen	2	10	5.0	1

RECEIVING

CLEVE	REC	YDS	AVE	TD
McCardell	3	47	15.7	1
Jackson	3	47	15.7	0
Metcalf	2	18	9.0	0
Carrier	2	8	4.0	0
Byner	1	14	14.0	0
Hoard	1	5	5.0	0
Kinchen	1	5	5.0	0

PASSING

PITT	COMP	ATT	PCT	YDS	TD	INT
O'Donnell	16	23	69.9	186	2	0
Tomczak	0	0	00.0	0	0	0

CLEVE	COMP	ATT	PCT	YDS	TD	INT
Testaverde	13	31	41.9	144	1	2

STEELERS 24, GREEN BAY PACKERS 17
DECEMBER 17, 1967

For One Day

The 1960s proved to be an up-and-down decade for the Steelers franchise. Following a couple of competitive seasons in 1962 and 1963, they descended into the bowels of the NFL, becoming one of pro football's worst teams. Conversely, the Green Bay Packers, the squad they were playing to wrap up the 1967 campaign, had just clinched their seventh division title in eight seasons and within the next month would capture their fifth NFL championship and second straight Super Bowl triumph. When the woeful Steelers marched onto the frozen tundra of Lambeau Field on this December day, it appeared to be a potential mismatch. But in the NFL, there's an oft-repeated rule: on any given Sunday, any team can beat another. This happened to be one of those Sundays when the cellar dwellers proved better than the front-runners.

Not surprisingly, a good portion of the announced sellout crowd stayed home rather than brave the temperature and the roads on an icy, rainy afternoon to see what almost certainly would be a one-sided affair. Ironically, those who stayed home would miss a very special homecoming for a former Packer. Kent Nix would start for the Steelers at quarterback after going along for the Packers' glorious ride the year before as a member of the practice squad. In his return to Wisconsin, he made the home team sorry it had let him go. Before Nix took center stage, the Pittsburgh defense drew first blood.

Three plays into the game, legendary Green Bay quarterback Bart Starr had a pass tipped by blitzing Pittsburgh defensive tackle Ken Kortas and linebacker Ben McGee—one of the very few players who would still be on the roster in 1972 when Pittsburgh won its first division title—intercepted the ball and returned it 21 yards for a touchdown and a quick 7–0 lead.

After the Packers kicked a field goal to cut the margin to four points in the second quarter, Nix led the team down the field as another Green Bay castoff, former first-round pick fullback Earl Gros, broke free for a 22-yard scoring run to make it 14–3. The Packers, no strangers to adversity, scored a touchdown of their own just before the half to make it 14–10. The Steelers had gotten off to a good start, but it seemed it was just a matter of time before they were overwhelmed by the superior Packers.

The second half began the same way as the first when Green Bay's third-string quarterback Zeke Bratkowski, who replaced backup Don Horn to begin the half, tossed an interception to the Steelers' only representative in that year's Pro Bowl, Marv Woodson. Though the Steelers couldn't cash in, moments later, another interception, this one by Ben Wilson, resulted in a Pittsburgh field goal to stretch the lead back to seven points.

As the third quarter was coming to an end, Bratkowki's rough day continued. With the Pack stuck at its own 14, the veteran quarterback went back to pass and was crushed by Pittsburgh linebacker Andy Russell. The ball flew out of Bratkowski's hand and into the arms of defensive tackle Chick Hinton, who took the ball in stride at the 27 and rumbled into the end zone for the team's second defensive touchdown of the game and a 14-point advantage.

Once again Green Bay would not roll over as Horn, who was the only Packers quarterback to enjoy success on this day, reentered the game and led the Packers to another touchdown to cut the lead to 24–17. When Nix tossed an interception with just under three minutes left in the game, it appeared that the Steelers' once-comfortable lead was about to evaporate.

Just when it seemed that they would collapse as they had done so much in the past, the Pittsburgh defense rose to the occasion, stopping the Packers on downs a minute later and giving the ball back to the Steelers' offense. Pittsburgh once again squandered an opportunity to run out the clock when Dick Hoak fumbled the ball after an 11-yard run, and the Packers recovered. Finally, Pittsburgh safety Paul Martha ended the drama when he picked off his fourth pass of the year to end Green Bay's comeback hopes and give the Steelers their most impressive victory in years.

The team hoped the season-ending triumph would be a harbinger of things to come, with Nix evolving into the Steelers' quarterback of the future. But the Steelers won only three games over the next two seasons and then selected Terry Bradshaw with the top pick in the 1970 draft. But for this memorable afternoon, with Nix at the controls in the icy rain at Lambeau, the Steelers took down the world champions, completing a brilliant day in an otherwise dismal decade.

BOXSCORE

TEAM	1ST	2ND	3RD	4TH	FINAL
Pittsburgh	7	7	10	0	24
Green Bay	0	10	0	7	17

TEAM	PLAY	SCORE
Pittsburgh	McGee 21-yard interception return (Clark kick)	7–0
Green Bay	Chandler 25-yard field goal	7–3
Pittsburgh	Gros 22-yard run (Clark kick)	14–3
Green Bay	Williams 29-yard pass from Horn (Chandler kick)	14–10
Pittsburgh	Clark 27-yard field goal	17–10
Pittsburgh	Hinton 27-yard fumble return (Clark kick)	24–10
Green Bay	Williams 25-yard run (Chandler kick)	24–17

RUSHING

PITT	ATT	YDS	AVE	TD
Gros	12	61	5.1	1
Butler	12	43	3.6	0
Hoak	8	18	2.3	0
Nix	1	0	0.0	0

GB	ATT	YDS	AVE	TD
Williams	10	73	7.3	1
Mercein	4	20	5.0	0
Wilson	7	6	0.9	0
Starr	1	0	0.0	0
Horn	1	-2	-2.0	0
Anderson	3	-4	-1.3	0

RECEIVING

PITT	REC	YDS	AVE	TD
Gros	5	35	7.0	0
Hoak	2	11	5.5	0
Butler	2	1	0.5	0
Wilburn	1	14	14.0	0
Jefferson	1	6	6.0	0
Hilton	1	5	5.0	0

GB	REC	YDS	AVE	TD
Williams	4	66	16.5	1
Fleming	3	52	17.1	0
Anderson	3	56	18.7	0
McGee	3	33	11.0	0
Dowler	2	23	11.5	0
Long	2	21	10.5	0
Wilson	1	6	6.0	0

PASSING

PIT	COMP	ATT	PCT	YDS	TD	INT
Nix	12	21	57.1	72	0	1

GB	COMP	ATT	PCT	YDS	TD	INT
Horn	11	19	57.9	154	1	1
Starr	5	11	45.5	90	0	1
Bratkowski	2	6	33.3	13	0	1

STEELERS 13, LOS ANGELES RAIDERS 7
DECEMBER 16, 1984

The Last Waltz

It had all come down to this. It was not just a game in Los Angeles against the playoff-bound Raiders trying to salvage a season in which the Steelers blew a three-game divisional lead with six to go, but a contest that could provide the franchise with one last day in the sun.

Over the previous 12 magical seasons, Pittsburgh had qualified for the playoffs 11 times, capturing four Super Bowl championships. By 1984, only a handful of players were left who had played a significant roll in the Steelers' dynasty: Mike Webster, John Stallworth, Bennie Cunningham, Donnie Shell, and Gary Dunn. The players who replaced Hall of Famers Terry Bradshaw, Joe Greene, Jack Ham, Franco Harris, Lynn Swann, Mel Blount, and Jack Lambert had kept the team competitive, making the playoffs in 1982 and 1983, but it was no longer a serious contender for a Super Bowl championship.

Still, 10 games into the 1984 season, the Steelers stood at 6–4 following an impressive win over an undefeated San Francisco team that would wind up winning the Super Bowl. With a three-game cushion over second-place Cincinnati, Pittsburgh was cruising toward a second straight AFC Central title.

But it suddenly became a tight race when the Bengals won four of their next five to pull within a game of the Steelers, who lost three games over the same period, including blowing a 10-point halftime lead to lose to Cincinnati in Week 15.

The Bengals appeared poised to catch the Steelers on the season's final Sunday. While Cincinnati would host the woeful 2–13 Buffalo Bills, the Steelers would fly west to face the gritty Raiders, who stood at 11–4 and needed a win to secure a playoff spot of their own. Since the Bengals also held the division tie-breaker against Pittsburgh with a better record against division opponents, the odds of the Steelers pulling out ahead in a division race they'd led all season suddenly appeared long.

"It's almost as if we don't want the darn thing," Steelers running back Rich Erenberg quipped before the important contest. "It's as if we're saying 'Here Cincinnati, take the championship.'" Fellow running back Walter Abercrombie had a more positive attitude. "They probably are a better team than us right now," he said of the Raiders. "But they can be beaten and we have just as good a chance as anyone of doing it."[1]

While Abercrombie was positive, the odds against Pittsburgh winning the division took a hit right before kickoff at the coliseum. The Bengals, whose game had started three hours earlier, had thrashed the Bills, 52–21. The stakes for the Steelers became very simple: win or go home.

With the season hanging in the balance, the Pittsburgh defense rose to the occasion, dominating the Raiders in the first half. But the Steelers had little to show for it, and a short Gary Anderson field goal proved to be the only points either team would score in the first three quarters. The Raiders' only scoring threat of the half was snuffed out when Shell—one of the only remaining stalwarts from the Steel Curtain defense—picked off a pass in the end zone. The Pittsburgh defense again came up big in the third quarter, stuffing Marcus Allen on fourth-and-one from the Pittsburgh 30 to halt a promising drive.

In a game with few big offensive plays, Abercrombie delivered the biggest play of the season. He took in a short Mark Malone pass at the Steelers 45 and darted through the Raiders' defense for a 59-yard gain to the Los Angeles 1. Fullback Frank Pollard then bolted into the end zone for the game's first touchdown to give the Steelers some much-needed breathing room.

Anderson capped another promising drive minutes later with a 37-yard field goal to make it 13–0 before quarterback Jim Plunkett finally put Los Angeles on the board with a two-yard touchdown pass to Dokie Williams with 3:30 left in the game to cut the Pittsburgh lead to six. The Raiders halted Pittsburgh to get the ball back, but once again the Steelers' defense came through in the clutch, clinching the game and the division title with an interception by Shell at the Pittsburgh 46.

Though the conclusion of the '84 season also marked the end of the greatest era in Steelers history, the dramatic win in Los Angeles provided one last taste of glory.

BOXSCORE

TEAM	1ST	2ND	3RD	4TH	FINAL
Pittsburgh	3	0	0	10	13
Los Angeles	0	0	0	7	7

TEAM	PLAY	SCORE
Pittsburgh	Anderson 26-yard field goal	3–0
Pittsburgh	Pollard 1-yard run (Anderson kick)	10–0
Pittsburgh	Anderson 37-yard field goal	13–0
Los Angeles	Williams 2-yard pass from Plunkett (Bahr kick)	13–7

RUSHING

PITT	ATT	YDS	AVE	TD
Abercrombie	28	111	4.0	0
Pollard	19	78	4.1	1
Malone	3	8	2.7	0

LA	ATT	YDS	AVE	TD
Allen	13	38	2.9	0
Hawkins	5	13	2.6	0
Wilson	1	8	8.0	0
Pruitt	1	-2	-2.0	0

RECEIVING

PITT	REC	YDS	AVE	TD
Stallworth	4	39	9.8	0
Lipps	3	32	10.6	0
Abercrombie	2	72	36.0	0
Erenberg	2	21	10.5	0
Cunningham	1	21	21.0	0
Thompson	1	6	6.0	0

RECEIVING

LA	REC	YDS	AVE	TD
Christensen	4	32	8.0	0
Barnwell	3	52	17.3	0
Williams	3	49	16.3	1
Allen	2	14	7.0	0
Branch	1	17	17.0	0
Hawkins	1	4	4.0	0

PASSING

PITT	COMP	ATT	PCT	YDS	TD	INT
Malone	13	23	56.5	191	0	1

LA	COMP	ATT	PCT	YDS	TD	INT
Plunkett	9	20	45.0	123	1	1
Wilson	5	13	38.5	45	0	1

STEELERS 27, CLEVELAND BROWNS 7
DECEMBER 7, 2006

Replacing Frenchy

He was known for three things in his career, two of them not particularly flattering. John "Frenchy" Fuqua was the player whom Jack Tatum of the Oakland Raiders blasted to set up the "Immaculate Reception" play in the 1972 AFC divisional playoff. Fuqua was also known as a very flamboyant dresser who once wore clear platform shoes with a goldfish in each heel.

The one truly positive thing Fuqua could be proud of in his career occurred on a special day in Philadelphia on December 20, 1970. That afternoon Fuqua etched his name in the Steelers' record book with a once-in-a-lifetime performance, rushing for 218 yards in a 30–20 loss to the Eagles. It broke John Henry Johnson's franchise mark set six years earlier and would stand for decades to come, becoming one of the most unique and revered records in the franchise's history.

For nearly 40 seasons, only a 190-yard effort by Barry Foster in 1992 seriously threatened Fuqua's record. It was the one mark that seemed like it might last forever, even in November 2006 when Willie Parker just missed the mark, tallying 213 against the Saints. It appeared Parker had just missed in his one and only challenge to Fuqua's record, but a little less than a month later, Parker would test it again on a frigidly cold night at Heinz Field.

Coming into the contest against their rivals from Cleveland, the defending Super Bowl champions were not enjoying a stellar season as they attempted to defend their crown. They had lost six of their first seven games, and though they righted the ship and entered the final month at 5–7, their playoff hopes were still slim.

In a nationally televised Thursday night contest against the perennially struggling Browns, the Steelers took control early and quickly eliminated much of the drama from the proceedings. As it turned out, Parker would provide enough on his own to make it a memorable night.

Midway in the first quarter, Pittsburgh embarked on what proved to be its longest drive of the year, with Parker rambling for 26 yards on five attempts to eclipse the 1,000-yard plateau for his second consecutive season. Moments later, quarterback Ben Roethlisberger fired a long pass into the teeth of a bitter wind that was caught by Nate Washington for a 49-yard touchdown pass and a 7–0 Steelers lead. Pittsburgh stretched the margin to 10 points early in the second quarter, and the lead held up until the half.

The Steelers turned the lights out on the Browns in the third quarter with a 91-yard drive that ended with a Roethlisberger touchdown plunge to make it 17–0. With victory secured, Willie Parker took center stage. The next time the Steelers had the ball, Parker ripped off runs of 39 and 11 yards and capped the drive with a short touchdown run. By the end of the third quarter, Parker already had 212 rushing yards, and Fuqua's record was in sight.

Realizing history was only six yards away, the chilled fans stuck around to see if they would get to witness Fuqua's name finally being erased from the record books. On Pittsburgh's next series, Roethlisberger gave Parker the ball on three consecutive plays that netted 11 yards to give him 223 for the night. Parker—who'd come to the Steelers as an undrafted free agent who'd never even started a game in college—left the game to a standing ovation after setting the all-time single-game record.

Almost as an afterthought, the Steelers tacked on another field goal, and the Browns scored a meaningless touchdown late to avert the shutout.

With Parker leading the way, Pittsburgh dominated the game, rolling up 303 yards rushing and a whopping 528 for the game. But while the game itself would soon be forgotten, Willie Parker would not, as he became the man who was finally able to push John "Frenchy" Fuqua from the record books.

BOXSCORE

TEAM	1st	2nd	3rd	4th	FINAL
Cleveland	0	0	0	7	7
Pittsburgh	7	3	14	3	27

TEAM	PLAY	SCORE
Pittsburgh	Washington 49-yard pass from Roethlisberger (Reed kick)	0–7
Pittsburgh	Reed 23-yard field goal	0–10
Pittsburgh	Roethlisberger 2-yard run (Reed kick)	0–17
Pittsburgh	Parker 3-yard run (Reed kick)	0–24
Pittsburgh	Reed 28-yard field goal	0–27
Cleveland	Edwards 45-yard pass from Anderson (Dawson kick)	7–27

RUSHING

PITT	ATT	YDS	AVE	TD
Parker	32	223	7.0	1
Davenport	14	62	4.4	0
Kuhn	1	16	16.0	0
Roethlisberger	3	4	1.3	1
Batch	2	-2	-1.0	0

CLEVE	ATT	YDS	AVE	TD
Droughns	5	6	1.2	0
Smith	2	4	2.0	0
Anderson	1	4	4.0	0
Wright	2	2	1.0	0
Vickers	1	2	2.0	0

RECEIVING

PITT	REC	YDS	AVE	TD
Holmes	4	81	20.2	0
Washington	2	67	33.5	1
Davenport	1	21	21.0	0
Tuman	1	18	18.0	0
Young	1	17	17.0	0
Kreider	1	6	6.0	0

CLEVE	REC	YDS	AVE	TD
Jurevicius	7	111	15.9	0
Edwards	4	86	21.5	1
Winslow Jr.	4	19	4.8	0
Droughns	2	23	11.5	0
Heiden	2	21	10.5	0
Northcutt	1	12	12.0	0
Vickers	1	4	4.0	0

PASSING

PITT	COMP	ATT	PCT	YDS	TD	INT
Roethlisberger	11	21	52.4	225	1	0
Batch	0	0	00.0	0	0	0

CLEVE	COMP	ATT	PCT	YDS	TD	INT
Anderson	21	37	56.8	276	1	1

STEELERS 16, DETROIT LIONS 13
SEPTEMBER 21, 1969

The Mirage

For the better part of 36 seasons, the Pittsburgh Steelers spent their time at the bottom of the NFL standings constantly trying to rebuild and find the perfect mix that would make them competitors for the league championship. It wasn't that owner Art Rooney didn't spend money to find the perfect coach for his team—hiring such football greats as Jock Sutherland, Walt Kiesling, and Buddy Parker—but while they occasionally had winning campaigns, they never had quite enough talent to get over the top.

Late in the 1960s, following a particularly bad five-year stretch in which the team posted an overall record of 18–49–3, the "Chief," as Rooney was known, gave more control of the day-to-day operation of the team to his son Dan, who tried his hand at rebuilding. After Dan offered the Steelers' head-coaching job to Penn State's up-and-coming Joe Paterno, and Paterno turned him down, the younger Rooney decided to go another way. Instead of offering money to a big name, he tabbed a young, relatively unknown Baltimore Colts assistant coach by the name of Chuck Noll to lead his franchise out of the cellar.

Noll's boss in Baltimore, Don Shula, knew the Steelers had made an excellent hire. "Chuck is very thorough," he said at the time. "He knows every phase of the game. What is important too is he has a real good manner with his players—firm, but gets along with them. He commands respect without being dominating. He is a fine young man and I hated to lose him."[1]

While it was great to hear such comments from one of the best head coaches in the league, three years earlier they had heard the same glowing comments from another legend, Vince Lombardi, about the last coach they had hired, Bill Austin, whom Noll was replacing after three less-than-stellar seasons in Pittsburgh.

As good as a coach as Noll may have been, without talent, he would go the same way as the unlucky 13 coaches who preceded him on the Steelers' sideline. It was as much about judging personnel as it was about coaching.

For the first draft pick of his tenure, Noll went for defense, drafting an unknown defensive tackle from North Texas by the name of Joe Greene. It was an unpopular pick, one that prompted a Pittsburgh paper to print the headline, "Who is Joe Greene?"

Now with an unknown coach and an unknown first draft pick, Steelers fans were questioning whether this was just continuing the long line of poor decisions the franchise had made. With doubts abounding, the Steelers opened the 1969 season at home against the Detroit Lions on a warm, sunny September afternoon.

This new era of Steelers football began much the same way as the previous ones. Running back Warren Bankston, the team's second draft pick the previous spring, fumbled, and the Lions recovered, setting up a field goal. Late in the first quarter, the Lions returned the favor, coughing up the football, and the Steelers recovered, leading to a field goal of their own. A nice drive by the Pittsburgh offense early in the second quarter resulted in another field goal and a 6–3 lead. In a game quickly being defined by turnovers, an interception by Pittsburgh defender Jerry Hillebrand sparked the game's fourth field goal to make it 9–3, and the score held up until halftime.

It certainly was not a pretty game, but after all they had seen in the past, Steelers fans had to be happy that the defense was holding firm and their hometown team had the lead, as slight as it was.

The Steelers had a chance to extend the lead early in the third quarter but missed a field goal. It was a missed opportunity that they would soon regret. The Lions cut the margin back to three points, then recovered Bankston's second fumble of the day midway through the fourth quarter and surged ahead 13–9 with the game's first touchdown with just over five minutes remaining.

The large crowd on hand was reliving bad memories. "SOS," short for "Same Old Steelers," was a common term in Pittsburgh during most of the first 40 years of their existence, and disappointment seemed to be descending once again.

When Pittsburgh got the ball back, the chances for a comeback didn't look good after a sack and incomplete pass forced them into a third-and-13 situation at their own 29. Quarterback Dick Shiner then hit tight end John Hilton with a perfect 23-yard strike for a critical first down. Moments later, receiver Roy Jefferson took the ball to the Detroit 36 on a 12-yard end-around, then the Steelers caught the break of the game. Shiner tossed a pass to Jefferson, which was short and tipped by Detroit's Mike Sweger. Luckily for Pittsburgh, Jefferson alertly caught the tipped ball before going out of bounds at the Lions' 6.

With time running out, the game's goat turned into the hero. Bankston, whose two fumbles had given the Lions 10 of their 13 points, took a handoff and broke three tackle attempts (including one by future Steelers defensive coordinator Dick LeBeau) and ran into the end zone with the dramatic winning touchdown, sending 51,000 previously doubting fans into exaltation. An excited Bankston tossed the ball into the crowd, which would cost him $100 for violating a new rule the NFL adopted just before the season began.

It was a fabulous beginning to the new era of Pittsburgh football. While the fans thought they were finally seeing the beginning of a winning tradition, for now it was just a mirage. The Steelers wouldn't win another game in 1969 and wound up losing their next 16 games. Over the first three seasons of the Chuck Noll era, they would win only 12 games, and it appeared as though nothing had changed. But this time, with Dan Rooney at the helm, the Steelers had both patience and a long-term vision. And when the rewards finally came, that dramatic opening win in 1969 proved to be much more than just a mirage.

BOXSCORE

TEAM	1st	2nd	3rd	4th	FINAL
Detroit	3	0	3	7	13
Pittsburgh	3	6	0	7	16

TEAM	PLAY	SCORE
Detroit	Mann 23-yard field goal	3–0
Pittsburgh	Mingo 27-yard field goal	3–3
Pittsburgh	Mingo 18-yard field goal	3–6
Pittsburgh	Mingo 40-yard field goal	3–9
Detroit	Mann 23-yard field goal	6–9
Detroit	McCullouch 12-yard pass from Munson (Mann kick)	13–9
Pittsburgh	Bankston 6-yard run (Mingo kick)	13–16

RUSHING

PITT	ATT	YDS	AVE	TD
Bankston	14	52	3.7	1
Gros	11	32	2.9	0
Shiner	4	13	3.2	0
Jefferson	1	12	12.0	0

DET	ATT	YDS	AVE	TD
Farr	10	35	3.5	0
Watkins	8	30	3.8	0
Triplett	9	13	1.5	0
Eddy	3	2	0.7	0

RECEIVING

PITT	REC	YDS	AVE	TD
Jefferson	4	47	11.7	0
Hilton	3	68	22.7	0
Wilburn	2	26	13.0	0
Bankston	1	2	2.0	0

DET	REC	YDS	AVE	TD
Farr	10	59	5.9	0
Sanders	4	43	10.7	0
Triplett	2	15	7.5	0
Malinchak	1	21	21.0	0
McCullouch	1	12	12.0	1
Eddy	1	10	10.0	0

PASSING

PITT	COMP	ATT	PCT	YDS	TD	INT
Shiner	10	26	38.5	143	0	1

DET	COMP	ATT	PCT	YDS	TD	INT
Munson	19	34	55.9	160	1	1

#42

Super Bowl XIII ½

In January of 1979, the Pittsburgh Steelers and the Dallas Cowboys put on quite a show in Miami for Super Bowl XIII. The teams were well matched, and the Steelers pulled out a 35–31 victory in what was considered the most exciting Super Bowl played to that point.

While NFL fans were still marveling at that game, they were thrilled when the league released the 1979 schedule. Nine months after their classic Super Bowl encounter, the Steelers and Cowboys would meet again in a regular season clash at Three Rivers Stadium.

It was the most-anticipated contest of the season, because it was not only a rematch of the previous Super Bowl but possibly also a preview of the next, with both teams favored to win their respective conferences again. As the highly anticipated game approached, the teams were living up to expectations. Dallas led the NFC East with a 7–1 mark, while the Steelers stood atop the AFC Central at 6–2.

While the defense had paved the way to a pair of Super Bowl titles in 1974 and 1975, by 1979, the offense had become explosive as exemplified by their 35-point outburst in the previous Super Bowl. By the time they played the Cowboys in this regular season matchup in '79, the Steelers had posted tallies of 42 and 51 points in a three-week period. However, the Pittsburgh defense had surrendered 103 points in its previous three games, opening it up to attack from a potent Dallas offense that had sparked four straight Cowboy victories going into the rematch at Three Rivers.

"Nobody will beat us like that," Hall of Fame defensive end Joe Greene said, not believing the Cowboys high-tech attack could disrupt the Steel Curtain defense. "To beat us you've got to run the ball down our throats. Very few teams will ever beat us doing what they do." And from the onset of this game, his words proved prophetic.[1]

With young Pittsburgh linebacker Dennis "Dirt" Winston starting for the injured Robin Cole, Cowboys coach Tom Landry decided to design his offensive attack around going after the inexperienced Winston. It turned out to be a mistake, as Winston had the game of his life.

With the young linebacker leading the way, the Pittsburgh defense was dominant in the first half. Dallas running back Tony Dorsett, formerly a star at the University of Pittsburgh, was coming off a string of four consecutive 100-yard games; in the first half he managed just 17.

Offensively, Pittsburgh fared no better as the Dallas pass rush battered Bradshaw, who by the half was nursing a bloody lip, a sore knee, and a numb left arm. Through it all, the Steelers' quarterback showed his toughness and endured.

While the Pittsburgh passing game was not firing on all cylinders, the running game stepped up. Early in the second quarter, the Steelers powered their way to the Dallas 1, where they faced fourth and goal. The normally conservative Steelers coach Chuck Noll decided to go for it, and the gamble paid off. "There was no way I was going to let him [Noll] go for a field goal," Bradshaw said later. Behind a key block from tight end Randy Grossman, Pittsburgh running back Franco Harris barreled into the end zone to give the Steelers a 7–0 lead.[2]

The Cowboys' offense immediately came back. Aided by a pair of personal fouls on the overly aggressive Pittsburgh defense, Dallas drove deep into Steelers territory and kicked a short field goal to cut the margin to four points. Symbolizing the growing tension between the teams, following the second Pittsburgh personal foul—a late hit by defensive back Ron Johnson—fiery Dallas assistant coach Mike Ditka angrily threw a football at Johnson. After a bold fake punt by the Cowboys failed late in the second quarter, the teams went to the locker room with the score 7–3.

In a game that had become a surprising defensive struggle, points were at a premium, and in the third quarter, a classic Pittsburgh play put the game out of reach.

After a nice punt return put the Steelers in Dallas territory at the 48, Bradshaw called what had been the offense's bread-and-butter play for most of the decade: "35 Trap." Running back Franco Harris took the handoff and blasted through a gaping hole in the Dallas defense—caused by defensive end Harvey Martin, who misheard the defensive play call—for a 48-yard touchdown run and a 14–3 Pittsburgh lead.

Usually in the NFL, an 11-point lead is hardly insurmountable. But on this day, the way the Pittsburgh defense was playing, it may as well have been 40 points. The Steelers held Dorsett to a mere 79 yards and midway in the fourth knocked Staubach unconscious on a savage sack by linemen John Banaszak and Gary Dunn. The score held up, and once again the Steelers had defeated the Cowboys.

On its cover the following week, *Sports Illustrated* dubbed the game "Super Bowl XIII½" and touted the contest as a preview of what was to come in Super Bowl XIV. The Steelers did their part, winning their fourth AFC title in six years, but the Cowboys couldn't make it back to the big show. After their fourth consecutive loss to Pittsburgh, the Cowboys lost three of their next four games and then were upset by the eventual NFC Champion Los Angeles Rams in the first round of the playoffs.

So while the October showdown between the two powerhouses wasn't a preview of another Super Bowl matchup, it was historically significant. For the Steelers, it was an affirmation that they still were the best in the league, a point that was driven home when they beat the Rams three months later for their record fourth Super Bowl title. And it reminded the Cowboys that while they were certainly one of the greatest teams in NFL history, in this era, they just didn't have what it took to take down the Steel Curtain.

BOXSCORE

TEAM	1st	2nd	3rd	4th	FINAL
Dallas	0	3	0	0	3
Pittsburgh	0	7	7	0	14

TEAM	PLAY	SCORE
Pittsburgh	Harris 1-yard run (Bahr kick)	0–7
Dallas	Septien 32-yard field goal	3–7
Pittsburgh	Harris 48-yard run (Bahr kick)	3–14

RUSHING

PITT	ATT	YDS	AVE	TD
Harris	18	102	5.7	2
Thornton	14	68	4.9	0
Bleier	1	8	8.0	0
Bradshaw	2	-5	-2.5	0

RUSHING

DAL	ATT	YDS	AVE	TD
Dorsett	19	73	3.8	0
Staubach	1	4	4.0	0
Newhouse	2	2	1.0	0
Laidlaw	1	0	0.0	0

RECEIVING

PITT	REC	YDS	AVE	TD
Stallworth	7	98	14.0	0
Swann	3	29	9.7	0
Harris	1	-1	-1.0	0

DAL	REC	YDS	AVE	TD
Pearson	5	89	17.8	0
Dupree	5	53	10.6	0
Springs	3	44	14.7	0
Dorsett	3	8	2.7	0
Pearson	1	9	9.0	0
Laidlaw	1	5	5.0	0

PASSING

PITT	COMP	ATT	PCT	YDS	TD	INT
Bradshaw	11	25	44.0	126	0	0

DAL	COMP	ATT	PCT	YDS	TD	INT
Staubach	11	25	44.0	113	0	0
White	7	17	41.2	95	0	1

The Postseason Waters

For the better part of its first 14 seasons, Pittsburgh's NFL franchise was among the worst in the circuit. The team had posted only one winning campaign and had never come close to entering the postseason waters.

After a 2–8 finish in 1945, owner Art Rooney, desperate for a postseason experience, decided to hire a Pittsburgh legend to lead his team. He tapped John Bain "Jock" Sutherland, who had gone 111–20–12 and won five national championships at the University of Pittsburgh. Not surprisingly, hiring a coach with Sutherland's reputation was not cheap. Rooney paid him $15,000, a huge sum for the time, plus 25 percent of the profits for any increase in attendance and an opportunity to buy fellow owner Bert Bell's share of the team if Bell opted out.

The price was high, but there were immediate dividends in 1946 as the team went 5–5–1 and saw an impressive increase in attendance from 15,000 to 22,000 per game; the following year, the improvement would continue.

After starting out 1–2 in 1947, the Steelers went on a six-game winning streak that included an impressive 35–24 win against their cross-state rivals, the Philadelphia Eagles, who would be their main competition for the Eastern Division crown.

When the two teams met for a second time in the next-to-last game of the season, Pittsburgh had a half-game lead and could essentially sew up their first division title with a win. But the Eagles were up for the challenge and shut out the Steelers, 21–0.

In the finale, Pittsburgh hosted the Boston Yanks, while Philadelphia played the Western Division-leading Chicago Cardinals. A Pittsburgh win coupled with an Eagles loss would mean the Steelers would venture into the postseason for the first time, either playing for the NFL championship or for the championship of the Eastern Division should the Eagles rebound with a win against Green Bay a week later. But if Philadelphia won its last two contests, and the Steelers lost their final game, the Eagles would win the division, while the Steelers would assume their normal position on the outside looking in.

To make the challenge more daunting, Pittsburgh would be without star tailback Johnny Clement, who was sidelined with a sore left shoulder. The SMU grad led the NFL with a 5.2-yards-per-rush average while becoming the first Steeler to pass for more than 1,000 yards in a season. Without Clement, Pittsburgh would have a more difficult time mustering up the offense to beat the Yanks.

Despite the setback, the 31,398 fans that crowded into Forbes Field for this contest had their hopes uplifted early thanks to the Steelers' special teams. With eight minutes left in the first quarter, defensive tackle Jack Wiley broke through to block a Boston punt, and Johnny Mastrangelo dove on the loose ball in the end zone to give the Steelers a 7–0 lead.

As the first quarter came to an end, kicker Joe Glamp gave Pittsburgh a 10-point advantage with a 30-yard field goal, and all eyes in Forbes Field turned toward the out-of-town scoreboard to see how the Eagles were faring. It was not the result they were looking for, as Philadelphia held a 7–3 lead.

Things got worse in the second quarter when the Yanks successfully pulled off a fake field goal for a touchdown that cut the Steelers' lead down to a precarious three points. The score remained 10–7 until the half, as did the Eagles' 7–3 lead in Philadelphia.

Early in the second half, the crowd at Forbes Field was whipped into a frenzy, though not with anything that was going on in the game they were watching. Public-address announcer Ray Downey relayed the message that Charlie Trippi had just scored for the Cardinals, putting them up, 10–7 over the Eagles. It was the beginning of a second half onslaught that saw Chicago score four unanswered touchdowns to win comfortably, 45–21.

Meanwhile, in Pittsburgh, the Steelers finally put some distance between themselves and the Yanks early in the fourth quarter when Steve Lach bolted in from one yard out to cap a 55-yard drive to restore their 10-point lead. Sutherland's troops were able to run the clock out for a 17–7 win, which—combined with Chicago's blowout win in Philly—gave Rooney his long-awaited postseason appearance.

But as it turned out, the Eagles had the last laugh. They beat the Packers the following week and then defeated Pittsburgh in the Eastern Division playoff game, 21–0.

Rather than the beginning of the first great era in Steelers history, their postseason appearance in 1947 would stand alone as a solitary achievement. Tragically, Sutherland was diagnosed with a brain tumor in the offseason and died soon after. The Steelers almost instantly returned to their pre-Sutherland doldrums, dropping to 4–8 in 1948, and they would have to wait 25 years before wading into the postseason waters again.

BOXSCORE

TEAM	1st	2nd	3rd	4th	FINAL
Boston	0	7	0	0	7
Pittsburgh	10	0	0	7	17

TEAM	PLAY	SCORE
Pittsburgh	Mastrangelo recovered blocked kick in end zone (Glamp kick)	0–7
Pittsburgh	Glamp 30-yard field goal	0–10
Boston	Golding 14-yard run (Maznicki kick)	7–10
Pittsburgh	Lach 1-yard run (Glamp kick)	7–17

#40

STEELERS 24, DALLAS COWBOYS 20
OCTOBER 17, 2004

Big Ben Comes of Age

Following a disappointing 2003 campaign in which the Steelers finished 6–10, the powers that be in the organization decided it was time to draft a franchise quarterback.

Since picking Terry Bradshaw in 1970, the franchise had made one other unsuccessful attempt to draft a quarterback with their top pick, Mark Malone in 1980. While Malone had modest success, leading Pittsburgh to the AFC Championship in 1984, he didn't live up to expectations and wound up being better remembered as a football analyst with ESPN than he did as a Pittsburgh quarterback.

Coming off their six-win campaign, they had the 11th pick in the draft and were hoping to grab either Phillip Rivers from North Carolina State or a hulking young man from Miami of Ohio by the name of Ben Roethlisberger, who had left school a year early for the NFL. When Rivers went to the Giants with the fourth pick, the Steelers feared Roethlisberger would be snatched up before they'd get a chance to pick him. They breathed a sigh of relief when the following six teams passed him over and then made Roethlisberger a Pittsburgh Steeler.

Tommy Maddox was the incumbent starter and would continue to be so while Roethlisberger slowly adjusted to the pro game. That timetable was pushed up much earlier, when Maddox was injured early in a 30–13 defeat to the Baltimore Ravens in Week Two. In the second game of his NFL career, the Ben Roethlisberger era had begun.

Roethlisberger completed 12 of 20 for 176 yards in his debut and won his first start a week later against the Dolphins in Miami. Victories at home against Cincinnati and Cleveland followed before his first real test: a contest in Texas Stadium against the Dallas Cowboys.

But the Cowboys looked strong in the early going, scoring a touchdown on their opening possession. Wanting to show he was up to the challenge, Roethlisberger quickly guided Pittsburgh on a 75-yard drive, highlighted by a 32-yard completion to Plaxico Burress. Roethlisberger and Burress connected once again for a five-yard touchdown pass to tie the game at seven.

After trading touchdowns in the first quarter, each team ended drives with field goals in the second and went to the half tied at 10. While Roethlisberger had been effective, the Cowboys' defense seemed to have figured out a way to slow down the Pittsburgh offense, and with Dallas keeping Roethlisberger and Co. at bay, the Cowboys built a 10-point lead late in the third quarter.

With only 18 minutes left in the game, trailing by two scores on the road with a rookie quarterback in only his fourth NFL start, the Steelers' odds for a comeback were long. But over those next 18 minutes, Roethlisberger would show he was no ordinary rookie quarterback.

He completed six consecutive passes to take Pittsburgh deep into Dallas territory and then hit tight end Jerame Tuman in the back of the end zone for a seven-yard touchdown pass to bring the Steelers to within three points.

As impressive as the drive was, it looked like it might be too little too late as Dallas stopped Pittsburgh at midfield with five minutes left in the game. With the Cowboys poised to put the game away, Pittsburgh linebacker James Farrior came up with a key third-down sack of veteran quarterback Vinny Testaverde and stripped the football. It was scooped up by Pittsburgh lineman Kimo von Oelhoffen, who returned it to the Dallas 24 with only 2:20 remaining.

On the next play, Roethlisberger hit Burress for 11 yards but was crushed by Dallas lineman Eric Ogbodu and lay on the field, writhing in pain. Roethlisberger would show the toughness that he would soon become known for, staying in the game and then completing his 11th straight pass, this one to Tuman that set Pittsburgh up at the Dallas 7 at the two-minute warning. Running back Duce Staley took the next handoff five yards, and reliable fullback Jerome Bettis finished off the drive with the go-ahead touchdown for a 24–20 lead.

The Cowboys had one last chance and drove to the Pittsburgh 30 in the waning seconds before a final pass was knocked away by Steelers defensive back Russell Stuvaints as time expired.

Quicker than expected, "Big Ben" had come of age, and the comeback victory vaulted Roethlisberger into the national spotlight. The wins kept coming, and when the smoke cleared, he led the Steelers to 14 consecutive victories, a record for a quarterback at the start of his career. He would go on to lead the Steelers to a pair of Super Bowl titles and undoubtedly become the franchise quarterback Pittsburgh had been looking for ever since the Bradshaw era had ended.

BOXSCORE

TEAM	1st	2nd	3rd	4th	FINAL
Pittsburgh	7	3	0	14	24
Dallas	7	3	10	0	20

TEAM	PLAY	SCORE
Dallas	Anderson 21-yard run (Cundiff kick)	0–7
Pittsburgh	Burress 5-yard pass from Roethlisberger (Reed kick)	7–7
Pittsburgh	Reed 51-yard field goal	10–7
Dallas	Cundiff 47-yard field goal	10–10
Dallas	Cundiff 39-yard field goal	10–13
Dallas	Johnson 22-yard pass from Testaverde (Cundiff kick)	10–20
Pittsburgh	Tuman 7-yard pass from Roethlisberger (Reed kick)	17–20
Pittsburgh	Bettis 2-yard run (Reed kick)	24–20

RUSHING

PITT	ATT	YDS	AVE	TD
Staley	18	93	5.2	0
Randle El	3	11	3.7	0
Roethlisberger	2	8	4.0	0
Bettis	5	8	1.6	1
Kreider	1	5	5.0	0

DAL	ATT	YDS	AVE	TD
Anderson	6	54	9.0	1
George	10	28	2.8	0
Johnson	1	13	13.0	0
Ward	1	11	11.0	0
Glenn	1	-3	-3.0	0
Lee	2	-3	-1.5	0

RECEIVING

PITT	REC	YDS	AVE	TD
Ward	9	76	8.5	0
Tuman	4	21	5.3	1
Burress	3	48	16.0	1
Riemersma	2	24	12.0	0
Staley	2	13	6.5	0
Randle El	1	11	11.0	0

DAL	REC	YDS	AVE	TD
Glenn	7	140	20.0	0
Johnson	6	61	10.2	0
Witten	5	39	7.8	0
Anderson	3	18	6.0	0
Bryant	1	22	22.0	0
George	1	4	4.0	0

PASSING

PITT	COMP	ATT	PCT	YDS	TD	INT
Roethlisberger	21	25	84.0	193	2	0

DAL	COMP	ATT	PCT	YDS	TD	INT
Testaverde	23	36	63.9	284	1	0

STEELERS 7, NEW ENGLAND PATRIOTS 6
JANUARY 3, 1998

On the Legs of Kordell

When the Steelers drafted Kordell Stewart in the second round of the 1995 NFL draft, head coach Bill Cowher wasn't quite sure what he had. Stewart was part of a new breed of quarterback: athletic and mobile, just as dangerous running the ball as throwing it.

Stewart's arm strength was never in question, exemplified by his legendary 64-yard "Hail Mary" bomb to beat Michigan when he was at the University of Colorado. What was in question was whether or not he was accurate enough with his strong throws, and whether he could pick up an NFL offense.

While many wondered whether he would ever start at quarterback for the Steelers, Cowher knew he had a fantastic athlete and was determined to find ways to use him any way he could. In Stewart's rookie season, he caught 14 passes as a receiver, averaging16.8 yards per catch, rushed for 80 yards, and completed five of seven passes. Because he was a triple threat, and no one knew quite where Cowher would play him, he was given the nickname "Slash." The downside of acquiring a reputation as such a versatile player is that it hinders the ability to become a star quarterback. Stewart was determined to be the exception. He would soon get his chance.

After Neil O'Donnell left in free agency following the 1995 season, veteran Mike Tomczak became the starting quarterback in 1996. But with Tomczak now 35 years old, Cowher took a gamble going into 1997 and named Stewart his starting quarterback.

In his first season as the starter, Stewart was both exciting and effective, throwing for more than 3,000 yards and 21 touchdowns while rushing for 476 yards and 11 more scores. Slash was now a star, and opposing defenses just didn't know how to prepare for him. And if they became too preoccupied with

Stewart, it opened up opportunities for running back Jerome Bettis, who had the best season of his stellar career with 1,665 yards.

Stewart and Co. won 11 games—including three in overtime—and captured the AFC Central title. Next up were the playoffs and a first-round encounter at Three Rivers Stadium with the New England Patriots, the defending AFC champions.

In what would become a memorable defensive struggle, the Patriots went into the contest at a disadvantage, playing without injured star running back Curtis Martin. As a result, the Patriots were limited to only 36 yards on 19 carries.

While the New England offense suffered, the defense kept the Patriots in the game. Unlike most of Pittsburgh's opponents that year, they found a way to stop the athletic Steelers' quarterback for nearly the entire game. In fact, Stewart only caused damage on one play. But it proved to be the play of the game.

Five minutes into the contest, from the New England 40, Stewart faked a handoff to Bettis and then took off around a key block by guard Will Wolford, sprinting down the sideline into the end zone for a touchdown and a 7–0 lead.

"It was a fake handoff to Jerome," Stewart said later. "Will Wolford did a great job pushing the defensive back out of bounds, and I just tippy-toed down the sidelines."[1]

After that, the New England defense bore down as their eight-man front line kept the Steelers' running game in check, limiting them to less than three yards per carry for the rest of the game. The Patriots dared the Steelers to pass, and the strategy worked. Stewart threw as poorly as the critics feared he would coming out of college, completing just 14 of 31 passes with an interception.

But the Pittsburgh defense was just as effective, limiting the Patriots to just a pair of field goals. Still, the lead was just a single point, and the game was up for grabs in the fourth quarter before Stewart directed the Steelers on their first long drive of the afternoon, marching to the New England 1 with just over three minutes remaining. Facing a fourth down with a field goal almost assuring them of a victory in this defensive battle, Cowher decided to be aggressive and go for the touchdown. Rather than giving the ball to the bruising Bettis, Cowher called for a quarterback sneak with Stewart, and New England linebackers Ted Bruschi and Todd Collins stuffed the Pittsburgh quarterback in his tracks, giving the ball back to the Patriots' offense for one more chance to win the game.

"I'm a young coach and I screwed up," Cowher admitted after the game. "I should have kicked the field goal. There is no way I shouldn't have."[2]

With both teams' seasons hanging in the balance, New England quarterback Drew Bledsoe drove his team near midfield before the Pittsburgh defense came up with the play of the season. Linebacker Mike Vrabel ripped through the

Patriots' offensive line and smashed into Bledsoe, forcing a fumble. Fellow linebacker Jason Gildon pounced on the ball, and Pittsburgh ran out the clock to escape with a 7–6 win.

"It was nice to help this team win," Vrabel said. "With the situation we were in, that was the biggest play. Hopefully there will be more to come."[3]

There would indeed be more to come for Vrabel, although not until he was a part of the team he'd just helped defeat. He went on to become a star for the Patriots and played a pivotal part of their three Super Bowl championships in the early 2000s.

For Stewart, it marked his first playoff victory and last one for four seasons as he quickly went from being revered to becoming one of the most ridiculed athletes in Steelers history. In one afternoon he encapsulated his entire career: on one hand, frustrating the Steeler Nation with his off-the-mark passing while, on the other, demonstrating his athleticism and versatility by using his feet to "slash" his team to victory.

BOXSCORE

TEAM	1st	2nd	3rd	4th	FINAL
New England	0	3	0	3	6
Pittsburgh	7	0	0	0	7

TEAM	PLAY	SCORE
Pittsburgh	Stewart 40-yard run (Johnson kick)	0–7
New England	Vinatieri 31-yard field goal	3–7
New England	Vinatieri 46-yard field goal	6–7

RUSHING

PITT	ATT	YDS	AVE	TD
Stewart	11	68	6.2	1
Bettis	25	67	2.7	0
McAfee	1	10	10.0	0

NE	ATT	YDS	AVE	TD
Shaw	10	22	2.2	0
Cullors	7	18	2.6	0
Bledsoe	2	-4	-2.0	0

RECEIVING

PITT	REC	YDS	AVE	TD
Hawkins	4	28	7.0	0
Thigpen	3	54	18.0	0
Johnson	3	28	9.3	0
Lester	2	3	1.5	0
Blackwell	1	14	14.0	0
Bettis	1	7	7.0	0

NE	REC	YDS	AVE	TD
Jefferson	9	104	11.5	0
Glenn	5	96	19.2	0
Brisby	3	37	12.3	0
Byers	2	1	0.5	0
Shaw	1	13	13.0	0
Gash	1	6	6.0	0
Brown	1	6	6.0	0
Cullors	1	1	1.0	0

PASSING

PITT	COMP	ATT	PCT	YDS	TD	INT
Stewart	14	31	45.2	134	0	1

NE	COMP	ATT	PCT	YDS	TD	INT
Bledsoe	23	44	52.3	264	0	2

STEELERS 13, BALTIMORE RAVENS 9
DECEMBER 14, 2008

A Fraction of an Inch

It had already been a very special season for the Pittsburgh Steelers. Although they'd faced a remarkably difficult schedule, had several key players miss time with injuries, and their offense—hindered by a weak line—ranked in the bottom half of the league, they stood at 10–3 going into a key divisional game against the rival Baltimore Ravens. A victory would secure an unlikely AFC North title.

This surprising success was due to an incredible defense, led by linebacker James Harrison and defensive back Troy Polamalu. The squad just missed pulling off the impressive feat of being ranked No. 1 in the league in fewest points and total yards allowed and had been the key component in propelling the Steelers to the brink of the playoffs.

Challenging them for the division crown were the 9–4 Ravens, who, like the Steelers, had an aggressive defense that was trailed only by the Steelers in yards allowed. Because Baltimore had lost to the Steelers earlier in the season in Pittsburgh, a loss in the rematch would eliminate the Ravens from the division race.

On a cold afternoon in Baltimore, where the Steelers had lost five straight games, the contest quickly turned into the tough defensive battle everyone expected, and the game was scoreless until the second quarter. Aided by a nice punt return, the Ravens kicked a short field goal to take a 3–0 lead, but Pittsburgh knotted the score on its next possession with a field goal of its own. As the half neared its conclusion, Baltimore retook the lead when quarterback Joe Flacco guided his team on a 14-play drive, capped by the game's third field goal for a 6–3 Ravens advantage.

Following consecutive three-and-outs on their first two possessions of the second half, the Steelers appeared to be following the script of their previous five trips to Baltimore, particularly when wideout Santonio Holmes fumbled after a reception at the Pittsburgh 21, and the Ravens recovered. They cashed in with another field goal for a six-point advantage that, on this day, seemed to be enough for victory.

Both defenses continued to dominate into the final quarter before the Steelers' offense finally got something going. Sparked by a 30-yard pass from Ben Roethlisberger to wide receiver Hines Ward, the Steelers drove into Baltimore territory and cut the lead in half with the fifth field goal of the game to make it 9–6.

Not about to be outdone, on the next possession, the Ravens drove to the Pittsburgh 27, eating up almost six minutes on the clock. With Baltimore facing third and eight, the Steelers made their biggest defensive play of the day. Linebacker Lawrence Timmons busted through the line to sack Flacco, forcing a fumble. Ravens running back Willis McGahee picked up the loose ball, but way back at the 41, pushing Baltimore out of field-goal range. Ravens punter Sam Koch then pinned the Steelers deep in their own territory at the 8, putting them 92 yards away from the end zone with only 3:36 left in the game.

The Steelers' backs were against the wall in a game in which they had been inept offensively all day. But this was the kind of moment in which great teams respond, the kind of moment that shows they're worthy of becoming a champion. And like a champion, the Steelers responded.

The possession started off with two 13-yard completions to Ward. Then wideout Nate Washington took over. He caught three consecutive Roethlisberger passes for 49 yards, including a clutch 16-yard catch on a third-and-10, when safety Ed Reed slipped, and took it to midfield.

As time was running down, Washington put the Steelers in field-goal position after a 24-yard pass to the Ravens 14. Ward then caught another pass for 10 more, giving the Steelers a first down at the Baltimore 4 with just over a minute remaining.

After an incompletion, Roethlisberger rolled to his left and then stopped and threw the ball to his right when he spotted Holmes just at the goal line. Holmes caught the ball with both feet in the end zone but was hit immediately by Reed. The officials ruled the ball didn't break the plane of the goal line. It appeared the Steelers would have to decide what to do on fourth and inches, but a replay review determined that the football had indeed crossed the plane. It overturned the officials' call, giving Holmes and the Steelers the go-ahead touchdown. As excited as the Steeler Nation was, the game wasn't over yet.

The Ravens quickly drove to the Pittsburgh 38 with 17 seconds to play, where Flacco launched a pass into the end zone for veteran wideout Derrick

Mason. Pittsburgh defensive back William Gay stepped in front of the pass and intercepted it to seal away both a satisfying victory and the division title.

Tomlin was ecstatic with both the final result and his offense's performance in the clutch, led by Roethlisberger. "[Number] Seven delivered, as he's done time and time again," Tomlin said. "I think a lot has been said about our offensive struggles, particularly in the last several weeks. One thing that is consistent is that when we need plays, when we have to move the ball, we have."[1]

And thanks to the heroics of the Steelers' beleaguered offense, they were able to prove the old axiom about football being a game of inches. On this cold day in Baltimore, that inch (or fraction of an inch) defined the Steelers' season and gave them the division title.

BOXSCORE

TEAM	1st	2nd	3rd	4th	FINAL
Pittsburgh	0	3	0	10	13
Baltimore	0	6	3	0	9

TEAM	PLAY	SCORE
Baltimore	Stover 28-yard field goal	0–3
Pittsburgh	Reed 31-yard field goal	3–3
Baltimore	Stover 26-yard field goal	3–6
Baltimore	Stover 28-yard field goal	3–9
Pittsburgh	Reed 30-yard field goal	6–9
Pittsburgh	Holmes 4-yard pass from Roethlisberger (Reed kick)	13–9

RUSHING

PITT	ATT	YDS	AVE	TD
Parker	14	47	3.4	0
Roethlisberger	4	21	5.3	0
Moore	7	16	2.3	0
Washington	1	6	6.0	0
Russell	1	1	1.0	0

RUSHING

BALT	ATT	YDS	AVE	TD
McClain	23	87	3.8	0
McGahee	6	18	3.0	0
Flacco	1	5	5.0	0
Neal	1	2	2.0	0

RECEIVING

PITT	REC	YDS	AVE	TD
Ward	8	107	13.4	0
Washington	5	76	15.2	0
Miller	3	26	8.7	0
Holmes	3	21	7.0	1
Parker	2	9	4.5	0
McHugh	1	7	7.0	0

BALT	REC	YDS	AVE	TD
Clayton	3	38	12.7	0
Mason	3	23	7.7	0
McGahee	2	15	7.5	0
Neal	2	15	7.5	0
Heap	1	23	23.0	0

PASSING	COMP	ATT	PCT	YDS	TD	INT
Roethlisberger	22	40	55.0	246	1	0

PASSING	COMP	ATT	PCT	YDS	TD	INT
Flacco	11	28	39.3	115	0	2

STEELERS 31, TAMPA BAY BUCCANEERS 22
DECEMBER 24, 1989

One in a Million

As the 1989 schedule neared its conclusion, the odds of the Steelers extending their season were long. On the other hand, they'd spent most of the season overcoming bad odds. At 8–7, they'd shown dramatic improvement over their 5–11 mark of the year before and had managed to turn their season around after a disastrous beginning that saw them lose their first two games to division rivals Cleveland and Cincinnati by a combined score of 92–10.

The Steelers went on to win eight of their next 13—including four of their last five—as Chuck Noll turned in one of the finest coaching performances of his career. To reach the playoffs, though, the Steelers still needed a very specific set of four circumstances to fall into place in Week 16. In horse racing terms, it was the equivalent of a superfecta, which usually has no chance of paying off. First and foremost on the Steelers' minds, however, was the only aspect they could control: they'd have to defeat the 2–8 Tampa Bay Buccaneers.

Things started out perfectly for the Steelers as speedy defensive back Rod Woodson returned the opening kickoff 72 yards to the Tampa Bay 17, and moments later rookie running back Tim Worley plunged into the end zone from a yard out to give the Steelers an early 7–0 lead. The Bucs, playing for nothing but pride, answered right back with a long drive and tied the game with a touchdown of their own. It was just a momentary lapse in what was to be a dominant game for the Steelers.

On the first play of the second quarter, colorful Steelers quarterback Bubby Brister tossed his first touchdown pass in almost two months, connecting with wideout Louis Lipps for a 79-yard bomb that made it 14–7.

After the Buccaneers closed into four with a 45-yard Donald Igwebuike field goal, Pittsburgh took control. A blocked punt led to another Brister-to-Lipps touchdown pass; then a Woodson interception set up a field goal that made it 24–10 at the half. Following a Tampa field goal late in the third quarter, the Steelers put the nail in the coffin. After Brister and Lipps connected for a key 28-yard gain on a third-down pass, Worley scored his second touchdown of the day to make it 31–13, and the Steelers were in the clear.

The Buccaneers tacked on a safety on a blocked punt and a long touchdown pass in the final minutes, but Pittsburgh hung on for a nine-point victory that kept its playoff hopes alive. Now all the Steelers could do was watch the scoreboard.

Amazingly as the final scores were coming in, Pittsburgh's once-distant hopes kept getting stronger. First, Kansas City's Nick Lowery kicked a 41-yard field goal with 1:31 left to give the Chiefs a 27–24 victory over the Dolphins, and New Orleans blew out the Colts, another AFC playoff contender, 41–6. To put the finishing touches of the incredible turn of events on this day, the Giants scored 17 unanswered points on the second half, overcoming a 14–7 deficit to defeat and eliminate the Raiders, 34–17.

It all came down to the Monday night game: if the Bengals won at Minnesota, they nailed down the last playoff spot, and if they lost, it would go to the Steelers. The Bengals roared back from a 22–7 deficit to cut the margin to a single point in the fourth quarter, but a late Minnesota touchdown sealed the victory and sent Pittsburgh to the postseason for the first time in five years.

What seemed like a one-in-a-million chance before the weekend began had actually panned out. It was an appropriate way to end one of the strangest, yet most memorable, seasons in Steelers history.

BOXSCORES

TEAM	1st	2nd	3rd	4th	FINAL
Pittsburgh	7	17	7	0	31
Tampa Bay	7	3	3	9	22

TEAM	PLAY	SCORE
Pittsburgh	Worley 1-yard run (Anderson kick)	7–0
Tampa Bay	Carrier 7-yard pass from Ferguson (Igwebuike kick)	7–7
Pittsburgh	Lipps 79-yard pass from Brister (Anderson kick)	14–7
Tampa Bay	Igwebuike 45-yard field goal	14–10
Pittsburgh	Lipps 12-yard pass from Brister (Anderson kick)	21–10
Pittsburgh	Anderson 32-yard field goal	24–10
Tampa Bay	Igwebuike 24-yard field goal	24–13
Pittsburgh	Worley 1-yard run (Anderson kick)	31–13
Tampa Bay	Safety punt blocked out of end zone by Cocroft	31–15
Tampa Bay	Carrier 39-yard pass from Ferguson (Igwebuike kick)	31–22

RUSHING

PITT	ATT	YDS	AVE	TD
Hoge	18	90	5.0	0
Worley	18	51	2.8	2
Brister	1	6	6.0	0

TB	ATT	YDS	AVE	TD
Tate	11	38	3.5	0
Sylvester	2	18	9.0	0
Harrishoward	1	17	17.0	0
Wilder	7	13	1.9	0

RECEIVING

PITT	REC	YDS	AVE	TD
Lipps	4	137	34.3	2
Mularkey	1	27	27.0	0
Hill	1	13	13.0	0
Worley	1	1	1.0	0

TB	REC	YDS	AVE	TD
Carrier	6	101	16.8	2
Stamps	3	34	11.3	0
Hall	3	33	11.0	0
Drewrey	2	24	12.0	0
Tate	2	20	10.0	0
Wilder	2	4	2.0	0
Harris	1	17	17.0	0
Howard	1	7	7.0	0
Peebles	1	4	4.0	0

PASSING

PITT	COMP	ATT	PCT	YDS	TD	INT
Brister	7	15	46.7	178	2	2

TB	COMP	ATT	PCT	YDS	TD	INT
Ferguson	21	41	51.2	244	2	1

STEELERS 37, GREEN BAY PACKERS 36
DECEMBER 20, 2009

The 500-Yard Passer

It had been a difficult defense of the Steelers' fifth Super Bowl crown. Injuries to key defensive players like Troy Polamalu and Aaron Smith hurt the team as the once-stalwart defense became a mere shell of itself.

The injuries were a major reason the team slipped into a frustrating five-game losing streak after a 6–2 start, losing the five games by a total of 22 points.

With their playoff hopes now in serious jeopardy, the Steelers hosted the Green Bay Packers at Heinz Field. The contest would become an offensive slugfest that would not only once again demonstrate how far the Pittsburgh defense had fallen but more importantly prove how impressive a quarterback sixth-year signal-caller Ben Roethlisberger had become. By the end of this contest, Roethlisberger would achieve something no other Pittsburgh quarterback had ever done.

Roethlisberger's counterpart on this day would be Green Bay's rising star Aaron Rodgers, who had freed himself from the shadows of the legendary Brett Farve, whom he'd replaced, and had become one of the best quarterbacks in football. He would finish the season with 4,434 yards and 30 touchdowns while throwing only seven interceptions, one of the finest seasons in NFL history. And like Roethlisberger, he was at his best on this December day in Pittsburgh.

While the sellout throng at Heinz Field believed this would be a defensive battle, that misconception was quickly dashed on the first offensive play of the game. Roethlisberger hit speedy rookie receiver Mike Wallace with a 60-yard touchdown bomb to put the Steelers ahead, 7–0. Completing the first of many rounds of anything-you-can-do-I-can-do-better on this day, less than five minutes later, Rodgers topped Big Ben when he found Greg Jennings on an 83-yard touchdown pass to tie the score.

Roethlisberger decided to slow things down a little, so to speak, on the next possession, completing five passes to push the Steelers to the Green Bay 2, where running back Rashard Mendenhall pounded into the end zone to make it 14–7. Both defenses recovered and kept the game scoreless for the better part of the next 15 minutes until Rodgers drove the Packers downfield with five completions before scrambling into the end zone from 14 yards out to tie the score midway through the second quarter.

After three consecutive fruitless drives, Big Ben did not want to be outdone by Rodgers. Completions of 27 yards to tight end Heath Miller and 33 to Holmes took the ball to the Green Bay 15, and three plays later Roethlisberger hit Mewelde Moore for another touchdown with 30 seconds remaining. The teams wrapped up an entertaining half of football with Pittsburgh up by seven.

In the third quarter, Jeff Reed nailed a 37-yard field goal to give the Steelers a 24–14 advantage, but everyone in the stadium knew a 10-point margin—and a Steelers losing streak—was anything but safe in a game like this. And sure enough, Rodgers and the Packers came right back with a touchdown to cut the lead to three. Minutes later Pittsburgh extended the margin to 27–21 with another Reed field goal, but with the Pittsburgh defense once again nowhere to be found, it was evident this game was going down to the wire.

Sure enough, with less than eight minutes left in the contest, the Packers took their first lead on a 24-yard scoring romp by Packers star running back Ryan Grant that made it 28–27, but as they had all day, the Steelers responded. A 54-yard pass to Hines Ward—who on this day would surpass the 1,000-yard receiving mark for the season for the ninth time in his career—set up another field goal to put Pittsburgh up by two points with four minutes remaining.

Knowing his defense was struggling and not wanting to give Aaron Rodgers so much time with which to work, Pittsburgh head coach Mike Tomlin called for a surprise onside kick. It didn't work, and Green Bay took over at the Pittsburgh 39, but Tomlin didn't regret his decision. "I wear that like a badge of honor," Tomlin said later. "That comes with the job. I don't live in fear."[1]

Rodgers took advantage, tossing a 24-yard touchdown pass to James Jones and then connecting on a two-point conversion to Brandon Jackson to give Green Bay a 36–30 advantage with just over two minutes left. After Pittsburgh's Stefan Logan bobbled the ensuing kickoff, the Steelers took over at their own 14, needing to drive 86 yards in two minutes to avoid a sixth straight defeat.

Following a sack, the Steelers faced fourth and seven at their 22. But in the face of adversity, Roethlisberger stayed in control. "Only one guy was talking in huddle, and that was Ben," Holmes said. "No other voice was spoken. No one had an opportunity to talk. We were dead tired." And, with the game on the line, Roethlisberger's poise paid off as he tossed a 32-yard pass to Holmes to give Pittsburgh both a first down and new life.[2]

Two receptions by Miller pushed the Steelers at the Packers' 19, but after two incomplete passes, only three seconds remained. They had one last chance to complete their comeback and snap the losing streak.

Roethlisberger, who had already surpassed Tommy Maddox's seven-year-old team record of 473 passing yards in a single game, dropped back and tossed the football in a perfect spot in the front corner of the end zone where only Wallace could catch it. Just barely in bounds, Wallace caught the pass as time expired to tie the game as the capacity crowd roared. Reed then won it with the point after as Pittsburgh finally ended its losing streak with a thrilling 37–36 victory.

The last pass not only delivered a much-needed Steelers' triumph but also put Roethlisberger in the record books. Those last 19 yards gave him 503 for the day, making him the first Pittsburgh quarterback—and just the 10th in NFL history—to pass the 500-yard mark in a single game.

The win sparked the Steelers to close out an up-and-down season with three straight victories to finish at 9–7. They missed the playoffs for the first time in three years, but with Roethlisberger now established as one of the elite quarterbacks in the NFL, the Steelers continued to be one of the NFL's most successful franchises.

BOXSCORE

TEAM	1st	2nd	3rd	4th	FINAL
Green Bay	7	7	0	22	36
Pittsburgh	14	7	3	13	37

TEAM	PLAY	SCORE
Pittsburgh	Wallace 60-yard pass from Roethlisberger (Reed kick)	0–7
Green Bay	Jennings 83-yard pass from Rodgers (Crosby kick)	7–7
Pittsburgh	Mendenhall 2-yard run (Reed kick)	7–14
Green Bay	Rodgers 14-yard run (Crosby kick)	14–14
Pittsburgh	Moore 10-yard pass from Roethlisberger (Reed kick)	14–21
Pittsburgh	Reed 37-yard field goal	14–24

TEAM	PLAY	SCORE
Green Bay	Finley 11-yard pass from Rodgers (Crosby kick)	21–24
Pittsburgh	Reed 34-yard field goal	21–27
Green Bay	Grant 24-yard run (Crosby kick)	28–27
Pittsburgh	Reed 43-yard field goal	28–30
Green Bay	Jones 24-yard pass from Rodgers (Jackson from Rodgers 2pt)	36–30
Pittsburgh	Wallace 19-yard pass from Roethlisberger (Reed kick)	36–37

RUSHING

PITT	ATT	YDS	AVE	TD
Mendenhall	11	38	3.5	1
Parker	6	22	3.7	0
Roethlisberger	1	7	7.0	0
Holmes	1	-2	-2.0	0

GB	ATT	YDS	AVE	TD
Grant	8	37	4.6	1
Rodgers	3	22	7.7	1
Jackson	1	1	1.0	0

RECEIVING

PITT	REC	YDS	AVE	TD
Ward	7	126	18.0	0
Miller	7	118	16.9	0
Mendenhall	6	73	12.2	0
Holmes	3	77	25.7	0
Moore	3	25	8.3	1
Wallace	2	79	39.5	2
Logan	1	5	5.0	0

RECEIVING

GB	REC	YDS	AVE	TD
Finley	9	74	8.9	1
Jennings	5	118	23.6	1
Nelson	4	71	17.8	0
Driver	3	76	25.3	0
Jones	2	36	18.0	1
Lee	2	4	2.0	0
Jackson	1	4	4.0	0

PASSING

PITT	COMP	ATT	PCT	YDS	TD	INT
Roethlisberger	29	46	63.0	503	3	0

GB	COMP	ATT	PCT	YDS	TD	INT
Rodgers	26	48	54.2	383	3	0

STEELERS 20, DALLAS COWBOYS 13
DECEMBER 7, 2008

Winning Ugly

Steelers head coach Mike Tomlin has always maintained he's not interested in "style points" when it came to football games. It doesn't matter if his team wins ugly, it just matters that it wins. That philosophy was never better displayed than in a game played on a frigid, windy December afternoon against the Dallas Cowboys, self-proclaimed to be "America's Team." Never was a win uglier—and yet, at the same time, so beautiful.

It had been a tough road for the Steelers in 2008, as they were plagued by a handful of key injuries while playing the league's most difficult schedule. Still, they came into the game with a 9–3 record riding a three-game winning streak, fresh off a victory in New England's Gillette Stadium, one of the toughest places to play in the NFL.

Dallas also came in having won three straight, led by their rock star of a quarterback, Tony Romo. Undrafted out of Eastern Illinois in 2003, Romo was developed by legendary coach Bill Parcells and quickly became the surprise of the league and one of its best signal callers. Against the Steelers, though, he would be facing defensive coordinator Dick LeBeau's array of zone blitzes, which had turned the Steelers into one of the best defensive units in the game.

As good as their defense was, Pittsburgh's offensive line had been under fire all year, allowing Ben Roethlisberger to become the second-most-sacked quarterback in the NFL. To make matters worse, the Steelers' once-proud running game was ranked 23rd in yardage despite ranking ninth in rushing attempts. Fittingly, this game would spotlight both of the primary characteristics of this Steelers team: the dominant defense and the struggling offense.

Things started ominously for the Steelers. After a Troy Polamalu interception of Romo gave the Steelers the football in Dallas territory, the offense quickly stalled, and kicker Jeff Reed missed a 45-yard field goal.

The defenses took over at that point. Both making game-changing plays in the first quarter, Steelers linebacker James Harrison and Polamalu stuffed Dallas running back Deon Anderson on a fourth-down run deep in Pittsburgh territory. Then Dallas's Bradie James forced Steelers tight end Heath Miller to fumble after a 15-yard reception.

The game remained a scoreless mess until Ike Taylor intercepted another Romo pass on the Dallas 22. Again the Steelers' offense was unable to cash in, but Reed connected on his second field-goal attempt of the day to make 3–0 with just under three minutes left in the half.

Dallas then responded with the game's first substantial drive, moving from its own 25 to the Pittsburgh 26 with five seconds left, before kicker Nick Folk tied the game with a 44-yard field goal as time expired in the half in what had become a very ugly game.

The Pittsburgh offense continued to struggle in the second half, but the Cowboys' offense would continue the momentum they established just before intermission. A Romo touchdown pass to wideout Terrell Owens gave Dallas its first lead; then the Cowboys stretched it to 13–3 when a field goal capped another long drive. The Steelers were staggering, but they weren't dead yet.

Roethlisberger quickly found his stride, hitting Santonio Holmes for a 47-yard gain, and in the opening seconds of the fourth quarter, the Steelers were knocking on the door at the Dallas 1. But four plays and a penalty later, they were still on the one, facing fourth and goal. The aggressive Tomlin decided to go for a touchdown, and running back Gary Russell was stuffed for no gain—and the Cowboys took over. It looked like the Steelers had blown their last opportunity to get back into the game.

The stout Pittsburgh defense held, and a 35-yard punt return by Holmes put the Steelers back in business at the Dallas 25. Another Reed field goal pulled them within 13–6, as the defense gave them an opportunity to tie by quickly forcing a three and out. Roethlisberger connected with wide receiver Nate Washington three times for 51 yards as Pittsburgh marched to the Dallas 6, where Big Ben hit Heath Miller in the end zone to tie the score with just 2:10 remaining. They hadn't played particularly well, but they'd played tough, and now it was a whole new ballgame.

After a short return on the ensuing kickoff, it appeared the Cowboys were content to try to run out the clock and win the game in overtime. A time-out then led to one of the most incredible plays in this long rivalry between these two proud franchises.

After a two-yard run by Choice that showed the Cowboys were intent on running out the clock, Tomlin called a time-out in hopes of stopping Dallas, get the ball back, and try to win the game. A perplexed Romo screamed to

Steelers linebackers LaMarr Woodley and Farrior, "Did you all really call a time out?" Farrior screamed back, "Yeah, what's your problem?" Farrior felt that their exchange "definitely added a little fuel to the fire." Indeed it had.[1]

On the next play, Romo, now irritated and looking to move Dallas down-field instead of playing for overtime, tossed a pass over the head of tight end Jason Witten that Steelers defensive back Deshea Townsend hauled in for an interception. Townsend then returned it 25 yards, diving into the end zone to give Pittsburgh a 20–13 lead with 1:51 left.

The stunned crowd was now in a frenzy, and after Romo tossed four straight incompletions on the ensuing possession, the fans roared even louder, taking it to another level as the Steelers exited the field with a victory in an ugly game they really had no business winning.

But Tomlin saw it differently. "Man, what a beautiful game," said the Steelers' coach. "I mean that. I just told the team that . . . you know people get too pre-occupied with style points. That was a beautiful football game. It's December . . . we will take the W."[2]

As surprising as the comment was coming from Tomlin, Steelers fans knew he was right. There is no ugliness in a win. To be sure, the Steelers earned no style points on this day, but there is nothing ugly about a win, particularly one as important to what had become a beautiful season.

BOXSCORE

TEAM	1st	2nd	3rd	4th	FINAL
Dallas	0	3	10	0	13
Pittsburgh	0	3	0	17	20

TEAM	PLAY	SCORE
Pittsburgh	Reed 24-yard field goal	0–3
Dallas	Folk 44-yard field goal	3–3
Dallas	Owens 12-yard pass from Romo (Folk kick)	10–3
Dallas	Folk 41-yard field goal	13–3
Pittsburgh	Reed 41-yard field goal	13–6
Pittsburgh	Miller 6-yard pass from Roethlisberger (Reed kick)	13–13
Pittsburgh	Townsend 25-yard interception return (Reed kick)	20–13

RUSHING

PITT	ATT	YDS	AVE	TD
Parker	12	25	2.1	0
Moore	5	22	4.4	0
Roethlisberger	5	17	3.4	0
Russell	4	6	1.5	0

DAL	ATT	YDS	AVE	TD
Choice	23	88	3.8	0
Romo	1	6	6.0	0
Owens	1	1	1.0	0
Anderson	1	0	0.0	0

RECEIVING

PITT	REC	YDS	AVE	TD
Washington	4	58	14.5	0
Moore	4	36	9.0	0
Holmes	3	82	27.3	0
Miller	3	20	6.7	1
Spaeth	1	6	6.0	0
Ward	1	2	2.0	0
Davis	1	0	0.0	0

DAL	REC	YDS	AVE	TD
Witten	6	62	10.3	0
Choice	5	78	14.6	0
Owens	3	32	10.7	1
Bennett	2	19	9.5	0
Williams	2	16	8.0	0
Curtis	1	3	3.0	0

PASSING

PITT	COMP	ATT	PCT	YDS	TD	INT
Roethlisberger	17	33	51.5	204	1	0

DAL	COMP	ATT	PCT	YDS	TD	INT
Romo	19	36	52.8	210	1	3

STEELERS 29, HOUSTON OILERS 24
SEPTEMBER 6, 1992

The Cowher Era

It had been 23 years since Dan Rooney had hired his first coach, Chuck Noll. Many questioned whether a young man with no head coaching experience was the best choice to turn around this losing franchise, but history—along with nine division titles and four Super Bowl championships—proved that Dan Rooney knew what he was doing.

Twenty-two years after he quietly entered the Steel City sports landscape, Noll exited just as quietly, announcing his retirement after the team's final game in 1991. Although the Steelers finished just 7–9 that year after back-to-back winning seasons, they were in the process of assembling the foundation for a second era of championship-caliber football, one that would be inherited—and accelerated—by Dan Rooney's second coaching hire. On January 21, 1992, that choice was announced and reflected his first: an unheralded assistant coach with no head coaching experience. And with that, the Bill Cowher era began.

Cowher was a hometown boy from Crafton, who first broke into the NFL as a player for the Cleveland Browns, just as Noll did. Also like Noll, he was an aggressive and intense player but just didn't have the talent for a successful career. Unlike Noll's quiet, unassuming personality, Cowher was a vibrant, enthusiastic, and very emotional presence on the sidelines. He was often in his players' faces, yet it had a positive impact. Whereas Noll shunned the spotlight, Cowher had a comfort level with attention and made it work for him.

The Cowher era began on the playing field in the 1992 opener against the defending AFC Central champion Houston Oilers, and the Steelers were heavy underdogs. No one was surprised when Houston, aided by a fumble return for a touchdown, quickly jumped to a 14–0 advantage. But with Pittsburgh about to punt the football back to the red-hot Oilers' offense, Cowher showed that the conservative, close-to-the-vest philosophies of the Chuck Noll era were no longer in place. With his head coaching career less than a quarter old and despite trailing by two touchdowns, he called for a fake punt, and punter Mark Royals completed a short pass to running back Warren Williams, which became a 44-yard gain and set up a short touchdown run by fullback Barry Foster to cut the Houston lead in half.

The teams traded punches for the remainder of what became an exciting half of football, and the Oilers took a 24–16 lead to the intermission. As Steelers fans would come to discover, Cowher was very good at making halftime adjustments, and in his first game, he and his staff made some defensive tweaks that wound up stifling All-Pro quarterback Warren Moon and the Oilers' run-and-shoot offense.

While the Houston offense scuffled, the Steelers narrowed the lead to two points with a pair of Gary Anderson field goals in the third quarter. Midway through the fourth, future Hall of Fame defensive back Rod Woodson picked off a Moon pass—one of five Pittsburgh interceptions for the day—and returned it 57 yards to set up quarterback Neil O'Donnell's second scoring pass, this one to tight end Adrian Cooper from nine yards to give the Steelers their first lead with just over eight minutes remaining.

There was still plenty of time for the potent Houston offense to score, but the determined Pittsburgh defense simply wouldn't allow it. With time running out and the Steelers trying to melt the clock, Cowher once again showed he could be both creative and unconventional in a pressure situation. An end-around run by receiver Dwight Stone went for 18 yards, giving the Steelers a key first down and allowing them to run out the clock to complete their upset victory.

The win set the tone for a surprising 11–5 campaign in which Pittsburgh captured its first AFC Central Division crown in eight years and began a golden era that saw Cowher lead them to eight division titles and the franchise's fifth Super Bowl championship in 2005. An exciting time period that all began on a September afternoon in Houston in 1992, with the start of the Bill Cowher era.

BOXSCORE

TEAM	1st	2nd	3rd	4th	FINAL
Pittsburgh	7	9	6	7	29
Houston	14	10	0	0	24

TEAM	PLAY	SCORE
Houston	Meads 15-yard fumble return (Del Greco kick)	0–7
Houston	Givins 11-yard pass from Moon (Del Greco kick)	0–14
Pittsburgh	Foster 1-yard run (Anderson kick)	7–14
Pittsburgh	Anderson 30-yard field goal	10–14
Houston	Del Greco 36-yard field goal	10–17
Pittsburgh	Graham 26-yard pass from O'Donnell (kick failed)	16–17
Houston	Givins 8-yard pass from Moon (Del Greco kick)	16–24
Pittsburgh	Anderson 25-yard field goal	19–24
Pittsburgh	Anderson 37-yard field goal	22–24
Pittsburgh	Cooper 9-yard pass from O'Donnell (Anderson kick)	29–24

RUSHING

PITT	ATT	YDS	AVE	TD
Foster	26	107	4.1	1
Stone	2	26	13.0	0
Hoge	3	8	2.7	0
O'Donnell	3	-5	-1.7	0

HOU	ATT	YDS	AVE	TD
White	13	100	7.7	0
Givins	1	4	4.0	0

RECEIVING

PITT	REC	YDS	AVE	TD
Graham	7	89	12.7	1
Stone	2	80	40.0	0
Foster	2	26	13.0	0
Hoge	2	19	9.5	0
Williams	1	44	44.0	0
Cooper	1	9	9.0	1

HOU	REC	YDS	AVE	TD
Duncan	8	98	12.3	0
Jeffries	7	117	16.7	0
Harris	7	49	7.0	0
Givins	4	42	10.5	2
White	3	24	8.0	0

PASSING

PITT	COMP	ATT	PCT	YDS	TD	INT
O'Donnell	14	23	60.9	223	2	0
Royals	1	1	100.0	44	0	0

HOU	COMP	ATT	PCT	YDS	TD	INT
Moon	29	45	64.4	330	2	5

STEELERS 37, CHICAGO BEARS 34
NOVEMBER 5, 1995

Through the Air

For the better part of two decades, Steelers football, when it pertained to offense, generally relied on a potent running game above all else. For the most part, Pittsburgh's passing offense was nothing more than a secondary complement. In 1995, that all changed.

Under the tutelage of offensive coordinator Ron Erhardt and with a stable of talented young receivers at his disposal, fifth-year quarterback Neil O'Donnell had become the single most dominant force in the Pittsburgh offensive attack.

The season didn't start out well for O'Donnell, though. He broke his hand in the opening contest against the Detroit Lions and missed the next four games. When he returned, the team was struggling. Despite the fact that they lost in his second game back, O'Donnell and his receivers were emerging into one of the most explosive units in the league. The Steelers pulled back to .500 before a trip to Chicago's Soldier Field, where the Steelers had never won in 11 tries.

Led by quarterback Erik Kramer, who already had 18 touchdown passes on the season, the 6–2 Bears boasted a strong offense of their own. With both teams' defensive secondaries riddled with injuries, the game quickly turned into a shootout, with two touchdowns by Pittsburgh running back Erric Pegram giving the Steelers a 17–10 halftime lead.

The lead quickly vanished when Kramer got rolling in the third quarter. A pair of touchdown tosses pushed the Bears ahead 24–17. The lead could have been more were it not for a handful of dropped passes by Kramer's receivers. Though the defense was struggling, the Steelers hung close, cutting the margin to four points with a Norm Johnson field goal late in the third quarter.

The Bears stretched the lead back to seven early in the fourth, but Pegram's third touchdown of the game knotted the score at 27 and set the stage for a race to the finish. Pittsburgh regained possession at its own three with just over six minutes remaining with a chance to take the lead, but an O'Donnell pass was tipped at the line of scrimmage and caromed into the arms of linebacker Barry Minter, who rumbled two yards into the end zone to give the Bears back the lead.

After forcing a quick Steelers punt on the ensuing possession, the Bears were poised to put the nail in the coffin when they lined up for a 44-yard field-goal attempt with less than four minutes remaining. Chicago kicker Kevin Butler had made his previous 16 field-goal attempts, but his kick hooked at the last moment and sailed wide of the goalposts, giving the Steelers new life. "I hit it good and I thought it was down," Butler said later. "It was an opportunity we had and we couldn't capitalize on it. It was definitely an important kick."[1]

O'Donnell took advantage and quickly led the Steelers down the field. With surgeon-like precision, he completed seven of 10 passes for 86 yards. With a little over a minute left in the contest, the Steelers faced fourth-and-six at the Chicago 11, and O'Donnell came through again, burning a Bears blitz to hit Ernie Mills for the game-tying touchdown. "You don't want to be third-and-eleven most of the time," O'Donnell said. "But I just tell the guys, give me some time and I'll find the receivers." He would find his receivers a franchise-record 34 times in this exciting game, which went into overtime after a last-second Hail Mary pass by the Steelers fell incomplete following an interception in the final minute.[2]

In sudden death, O'Donnell continued his assault on the Bears' secondary, taking the Steelers inside the Chicago 10 thanks to two more third-down conversions. Not wanting to risk losing the ball on a turnover, Bill Cowher called on Norm Johnson, and the veteran kicker successfully connected from 24 yards out to break Pittsburgh's Windy City losing streak in Chicago with an exciting 37–34 win.

"This was a very big win," said O'Donnell, who finished with 341 yards passing. "We're on the road and no one gave us a chance to win. It's just a start of a lot of good things to happen."[3]

O'Donnell's statement proved prophetic as the Steelers went on to win six straight to capture the AFC Central title and reach the Super Bowl for the first time in 16 years.

It turned out to be a season filled with big games, but it was their aerial-show victory in Chicago that set the tone for the championship run. And perhaps appropriately, it was a game that was won through the air, representing the new brand of Steelers football.

BOXSCORE

TEAM	1st	2nd	3rd	4th	OT	FINAL
Pittsburgh	0	17	3	14	3	37
Chicago	3	7	14	10	0	34

TEAM	PLAY	SCORE
Chicago	Butler 40-yard field goal	0–3
Pittsburgh	Pegram 1-yard run (Johnson kick)	7–3
Chicago	Conway 6-yard pass from Kramer (Butler kick)	7–10
Pittsburgh	Johnson 40-yard field goal	10–10
Pittsburgh	Pegram 7-yard pass from O'Donnell (Johnson kick)	17–10
Chicago	Carter 12-yard pass from Kramer (Butler kick)	17–17
Chicago	Wetnight 14-yard pass from Kramer (Butler kick)	17–24
Pittsburgh	Johnson 46-yard field goal	20–24
Chicago	Butler 27-yard field goal	20–27
Pittsburgh	Pegram 6-yard run (Johnson kick)	27–27
Chicago	Minter 2 interception return (Butler kick)	34–27
Pittsburgh	Mills 11-yard pass from O'Donnell (Johnson kick)	34–34
Pittsburgh	Johnson 24-yard field goal	37–34

RUSHING

PITT	ATT	YDS	AVE	TD
Pegram	24	61	2.5	2
Williams	4	13	3.3	0
Mills	1	6	6.0	0
Stewart	1	2	2.0	0
O'Donnell	1	2	2.0	0
Thigpen	1	1	1.0	0

RUSHING

CHI	ATT	YDS	AVE	TD
Salaam	21	63	3.0	0
Green	4	20	5.0	0
Johnson	2	18	9.0	0
Conway	1	18	18.0	0
Kramer	1	1	1.0	0

RECEIVING

PITT	REC	YDS	AVE	TD
Thigpen	10	108	10.8	0
Pegram	6	37	6.2	1
Johnson	4	52	13.0	0
Williams	4	17	4.3	0
Mills	3	49	16.3	1
Hastings	3	32	10.7	0
Hayes	2	14	7.0	0
Stewart	1	27	27.0	0
Bruener	1	5	5.0	0

CHI	REC	YDS	AVE	TD
Graham	5	111	22.2	0
Conway	4	55	13.8	1
Wetnight	2	21	10.5	1
Jennings	2	15	7.5	0
Timpson	1	14	14.0	0
Carter	1	12	12.0	1

PASSING

PITT	COMP	ATT	PCT	YDS	TD	INT
O'Donnell	34	52	65.3	341	2	2

CHI	COMP	ATT	PCT	YDS	TD	INT
Kramer	15	28	53.5	228	3	3

STEELERS 19, ST. LOUIS CARDINALS 7
DECEMBER 2, 1962

The 1,000-Yard Barrier

As the Pittsburgh Steelers celebrated their 30th season in the NFL, they still had never had a running back rush for more than 1,000 yards in a season. For that matter, no running back had topped even 800 yards. Going into 1962, the franchise record for most yards rushing in a campaign was held by a forgettable, diminutive five-foot-nine running back named Tom Tracy, who picked up 794 yards in 1958.

Tracy's modest record would be shattered four years later, when John Henry Johnson, a 33-year-old veteran not only topped Tracy's mark but etched his name into franchise history when he became the first Steeler ever to rush for over 1,000 yards in a single season.

Johnson was a punishing runner out of St. Mary's College and Arizona State who followed head coach Buddy Parker from Detroit, coming to Pittsburgh via a trade with the Lions in 1960. Known as something of a troublemaker in Detroit, Johnson had fallen out of favor with the Lions' front office and was dealt for the Steelers' first-round draft picks in 1961 and 1962. It was a high price, but it paid off as Johnson rushed for 787 yards in '61, falling just short of Tracy's record. It was a preview of what was to come in 1962.

After starting off with a mere 21 yards in a 45–7 thrashing at the hands of his former team in the opener, Johnson got rolling. He rushed for 113 yards in a week three loss to the New York Giants, the first of three consecutive 100-yard games. But as successful as Johnson had been, the Steelers struggled to a 3–4 mark at the season's midpoint.

Pittsburgh bounced back to win three of the next four games and stood at 6–5 going into the home finale against the St. Louis Cardinals, a team the

Steelers had defeated 11 consecutive times. By now, Johnson had amassed 918 yards, toppling Tracy's record, and had his sights set on the four-digit mark.

While Johnson was pursuing history, the Steelers were shooting for a trip to the postseason. With a win and losses by Cleveland and Washington, Pittsburgh would move into second place in the Eastern Division with only two games to play. If they could hang in second, they would play in the second postseason game in the history of the franchise, an exhibition contest called the Playoff Bowl, which pitted the second-place teams from each division in Miami's Orange Bowl.

Against the Cardinals, the Pittsburgh offense flourished, piling up 412 yards, but the Steelers were unable to punch the football into the end zone and repeatedly had to settle for field-goal attempts. Kicker Lou Michaels made four on the day but also missed four, including a block that gave the Cardinals a chance to take an early lead. St. Louis drove to the Pittsburgh 4, but the Steelers' Dick Haley forced a fumble that was scooped up by John Reger, ending the Cardinals threat.

Not long after, Pittsburgh's defense provided the team's only points of the first half when second-year safety Willie Daniel made a leaping interception of a Charley Johnson pass and zigzagged through the St. Louis offense from 49 yards to give Pittsburgh an early 7–0 lead.

In the second quarter, the Cardinals once again threatened but again were halted by a fumble, recovered by the Steelers' Ernie Stautner. The Steelers returned the favor when a 34-yard touchdown pass from Ed Brown to Buddy Dial was wiped out on a holding call. With the mistakes piling up, the Steelers' 7–0 lead endured. And though the Pittsburgh offense had been successful in moving the ball, St. Louis was keeping Johnson in check, limiting him to just 24 yards in the first half.

Three Michaels field goals pushed the margin to 16–0 in the fourth quarter. Then the Cardinals scored a late touchdown to avoid a shutout. With victory in his grasp, Parker decided it was time for Johnson to grind out the lock and write himself into Steelers history. The hulking fullback began to rip through the Cardinals' tiring defense, helping the Steelers drive deep into St. Louis territory to set up another Michaels field goal. Along the way, Johnson finally did it, finishing the contest with 98 and lifting his season total to 1,016.

He ended the campaign with 1,141 yards and two seasons later broke the 1,000-yard plateau once again at the age of 35. Those two seasons with the Steelers helped propel his election into the Pro Football Hall of Fame in 1987, a fitting achievement for a fantastic player and a pioneer in Pittsburgh Steelers history.

BOXSCORE

TEAM	1st	2nd	3rd	4th	FINAL
St. Louis	0	0	0	7	7
Pittsburgh	7	0	6	6	19

TEAM	PLAY	SCORE
Pittsburgh	Daniel 49-yard interception return (Michaels kick)	0–7
Pittsburgh	Michaels 35-yard field goal	0–10
Pittsburgh	Michaels 36-yard field goal	0–13
Pittsburgh	Michaels 23-yard field goal	0–16
St. Louis	Randle El 12-yard pass from Johnson (Perry kick)	7–16
Pittsburgh	Michaels 10-yard field goal	7–19

RUSHING

PITT	ATT	YDS	AVE	TD
Johnson	17	98	5.8	0
Tracy	7	72	10.3	0
Hoak	14	65	4.6	0
Ferguson	2	3	1.5	0

STL	ATT	YDS	AVE	TD
Crow	9	31	3.4	0
Childress	5	14	2.8	0
Hammack	3	13	4.3	0
Johnson	1	0	0.0	0

RECEIVING

PITT	REC	YDS	AVE	TD
Dial	7	186	26.5	0
Carpenter	4	52	13.0	0
Johnson	1	8	8.0	0

RECEIVING

STL	REC	YDS	AVE	TD
Conrad	7	106	15.1	0
Crow	4	80	20.0	0
Randle	4	49	12.3	1
Anderson	2	22	11.0	0
Hammack	1	10	10.0	0

PASSING

PITT	COMP	ATT	PCT	YDS	TD	INT
Brown	12	27	44.4	246	0	1

STL	COMP	ATT	PCT	YDS	TD	INT
Johnson	17	37	45.9	257	1	2
Etcheverry	1	1	100.0	10	0	0

STEELERS 21, CHICAGO BEARS 9
DECEMBER 11, 2005

The Wheels on the Bus

It had been an emotional time for the Pittsburgh Steelers following their 41–27 loss to the New England Patriots in the 2004 AFC Championship game. After winning 14 straight regular season games to finish 15–1, they hoped the season would end with their leader, Jerome Bettis, finally getting a chance to play in a Super Bowl after so many close misses in his 12-year career. But it was not to be, and Bettis considered retirement. His teammates, especially receiver Hines Ward, were distraught that this might be the end of the line for the man they affectionately called "The Bus" and they'd been unable to give him the title he desired.

After thinking it over in the offseason, Bettis decided to give it one last try in 2005. He would do so in a different role, however: as a backup to new starter Willie Parker.

Despite the fact that Bettis was no longer the primary weapon, the Pittsburgh ground game was off and running, helping lead the Steelers to a 7–2 mark. With the season looking nearly as promising as the one before, the rug slipped out from underneath the Steelers as they lost consecutive games to the Ravens, Colts, and Bengals. Now at 7–5, they needed to win their final four games to return to the postseason for a shot to give Bettis his title. Their first hurdle would be the team with the stingiest defense in the league, the Chicago Bears.

At 9–3, the Bears were atop the NFC Central Division and had yielded less than 10 points in 7 of their 12 games, never permitting more than 20. The Steelers' work was cut out for them.

As tough as Chicago's defense was, Steelers head coach Bill Cowher felt his team could move the ball against the Bears, and they set out to prove it early on. Following a defensive stop by the Steelers on the Bears' first possession,

Pittsburgh took over on its own 34. After a loss of one on his first carry, Parker took a short screen pass from Ben Roethlisberger and broke free for 45 yards. On another screen moments later, Ward slashed 14 yards through the Bears' defense, breaking several tackles for the first score of the day and a 7–0 Pittsburgh lead.

Bears quarterback Kyle Orton, who had been steady if unspectacular for Chicago, responded by taking his team on a 12-play drive to the Pittsburgh 3. With snow starting to fall, Steelers linebacker Clark Haggans burst through the line on a misdirection play, sacking Orton for an eight-yard loss. Chicago was forced to settle for a Robbie Gould 29-yard field goal to cut the lead to 7–3.

Early in the second quarter, Roethlisberger completed a short two-yard pass to running back Verron Haynes on a third and three. The Bears declined an offensive pass interference call on Hines Ward on the play, opting to make the Steelers face fourth and one. Haynes caught another short pass, spinning through several tackles for 16 yards and a key first down. With the aggressive Chicago defense back on its heels once again, the Steelers' confidence was growing. After an 11-yard run by Parker, Bettis did what he did best and barreled into the end zone from a yard out to give Pittsburgh a 14–3 lead that held until the half.

As the teams took the field to start the third quarter, the light snow turned into a virtual whiteout, taking visibility down to just a few feet and turning the field into an ivory quagmire. Cowher decided to have Bettis carry the load in these conditions, though he'd only managed 22 rushing yards in his previous two games.

With the running game pacing the attack, passing lanes opened up and Roethlisberger hit two clutch third-down tosses to Antwaan Randle El and Quincy Morgan to put the Steelers inside the Chicago 10. It was at that point the man called "The Bus" showed the Bears what power football was meant to be. After a three-yard run from the 8, Bettis took off around right tackle. At the 2 he encountered Bears linebacker Brian Urlacher, one of the toughest and best defensive players in the game. Bettis crashed into him head-on, plowing through Urlacher and into the end zone for a touchdown to make it 21–3. An excited Bettis later quipped into sideline cameras: "They ain't so tough. It's smash mouth football baby, Pittsburgh style."[1]

As the fourth quarter began with the field blanketed with snow, Orton scored a touchdown, and the Bears pulled within 12 points, though they missed the extra point. Bettis and Parker kept pounding the Chicago defense—including a 39-yard scamper by Bettis, his longest since 2002—and the Steelers' defense dug in to prevent the Bears from scoring again, allowing the Steelers to wrap up their important 21–9 victory.

Bettis finished the contest with a game-high 101 yards on 17 carries. It was his first 100-yard game of the year and, as it turned out, the last of his career. Though he hadn't played much all season, Bettis had come through when the Steelers needed him most.

With "The Bus" leading the way, the Steelers grabbed the momentum they were looking for. They won their final four games and carried the swing into the playoffs and all the way to the Super Bowl. There were many memorable moments along the way, but none would have been possible without Bettis's gritty performance in the snow against Chicago—an appropriate curtain call for one of the greatest players in franchise history.

BOXSCORE

TEAM	1st	2nd	3rd	4th	FINAL
Chicago	3	0	0	6	9
Pittsburgh	7	7	7	0	21

TEAM	PLAY	SCORE
Pittsburgh	Ward 14-yard pass from Roethlisberger (Reed kick)	0–7
Chicago	Gould 29-yard field goal	3–7
Pittsburgh	Bettis 1-yard run (Reed kick)	3–14
Pittsburgh	Bettis 5-yard run (Reed kick)	3–21
Chicago	Jones 1-yard run (Gould kick)	9–21

RUSHING

PITT	ATT	YDS	AVE	TD
Bettis	17	101	5.9	2
Parker	21	68	3.2	0
Kreider	1	12	12.0	0
Haynes	4	8	2.0	0
Randle El	1	3	3.0	0
Roethlisberger	2	-2	-1.0	0

RUSHING

CHI	ATT	YDS	AVE	TD
Jones	14	72	5.1	1
Orton	3	8	2.7	0

RECEIVING

PITT	REC	YDS	AVE	TD
Ward	3	27	9.0	1
Parker	2	45	22.5	0
Haynes	2	29	14.5	0
Wilson	2	29	14.5	0
Randle El	2	28	14.0	0
Morgan	1	10	10.0	0
Kreider	1	5	5.0	0

CHI	REC	YDS	AVE	TD
Muhammad	8	91	11.4	0
Jones	4	23	5.8	0
Berrian	1	43	43.0	0
Clark	1	27	27.0	0
Gage	1	11	11.0	0
Johnson	1	7	7.0	0
Wade	1	5	5.0	0

PASSING

PITT	COMP	ATT	PCT	YDS	TD	INT
Roethlisberger	13	20	65.0	173	1	0

CHI	COMP	ATT	PCT	YDS	TD	INT
Orton	17	35	48.6	207	0	0

STEELERS 31, CINCINNATI BENGALS 17
JANUARY 6, 2006

We Dey

It was one of the lowest points in modern Steelers history. They'd followed up a magnificent 15–1 campaign in 2004 with a 7–2 start in 2005, but then everything came to a screeching halt with a troubling three-game losing streak. The last of Pittsburgh's trio of defeats came against their bitter rivals from Cincinnati, and, even worse, it was a heartbreaking loss in Pittsburgh. The loss dropped the Steelers to 7–5, putting them in a position where they had to win the final four games to make the playoffs.

Cincinnati fans who had traveled east alongside the Ohio River to take in the game wasted no time taunting Steelers fans once the Bengals wrapped up the victory. They repeated their traditional—and, to opposing fans, irritating—chant: "Who dey think gonna beat dem Bengals?!" Amidst the Bengals' euphoria, Cincinnati wide receiver T. J. Houshmandzadeh mimed shining his shoes with a Terrible Towel on the Heinz Field turf—an act that both the Steelers and their fans knew could not be ignored. Since this was the final time the teams would meet in 2005, it appeared the moment would have to burn in the Steelers' minds for another year until they had a chance to exact revenge. As it turned out, they'd have their chance much sooner.

Pittsburgh reeled off four consecutive victories to end the season with an 11–5 record, and they captured the final wild card spot. As it turned out, the seedings dictated that Pittsburgh would travel to Cincinnati to face the AFC North champion Bengals in the first round of the playoffs, giving the Steelers the chance to avenge the loss to the Bengals.

Beating the Bengals in Cincinnati wouldn't be easy. Led by quarterback Carson Palmer, who had become one of the elite quarterbacks in the league with a 101.1 passer rating, and Rudy Johnson, who rushed for 1,458 yards,

Cincinnati had developed an explosive offense that was fourth in the league in points scored. The Bengals still were vulnerable, though, reflected by one of the league's worst defenses and blowout losses in the final two weeks of the season that had cost them a first-round bye.

Despite the poor ending to their season, Cincinnati began this playoff game like it was a continuation of their last victory against the Steelers. On their second play from scrimmage, Palmer hit wideout Chris Henry along the sideline for a 66-yard gain, and the sellout crowd at Paul Brown Stadium went instantly crazy. But in the moments after the play, the roar quieted as the fans saw Palmer lying on the field, clutching his knee. Attempting to protect his quarterback, Cincinnati guard Eric Steinbach had blocked Pittsburgh defensive tackle Kimo von Oelhoffen into Palmer's leg. The result was a torn ACL and MCL for Palmer, whose day—and season—was over.

At first, it didn't seem like losing Palmer had any effect. Backup Jon Kitna stepped in and led the Bengals to a 10–0 lead and then answered a Pittsburgh touchdown early in the second quarter with one of their own to maintain their 10-point lead. Even without Palmer, the Cincinnati offense looked unstoppable, and the Steelers appeared overwhelmed.

The Steelers faced much adversity in 2005. And once again in an adverse situation, they responded. A 54-yard pass from Ben Roethlisberger to Cedric Wilson brought the Steelers to life, and moments later a Hines Ward touchdown catch pulled Pittsburgh within three points just before the half.

The Bengals squandered a chance to pad their cushion on the first possession of the third quarter when a bad center snap on a short field-goal attempt gave the ball back to the Steelers. A long pass-interference penalty on Cincinnati pushed them to the Bengals 5, where Jerome Bettis powered into the end zone to give the Steelers a 21–17 lead.

With the momentum now completely shifted, Pittsburgh defensive coordinator Dick LeBeau started to blitz Kitna more often, which kept him out of rhythm the rest of the way. Two quick sacks and a Kitna fumble gave the Steelers the ball back, and they delivered the knockout punch.

On third and three from the Cincinnati 43, Pittsburgh wide receiver Antwaan Randle El took a direct snap from center, ran to his left, and then stopped and threw a lateral across the field to Roethlisberger, who caught the ball and launched a long pass to wide-open Cedric Wilson. With no defender within 15 yards, Wilson strolled into the end zone for a touchdown and an 11-point Pittsburgh lead that silenced the Bengals' home crowd once and for all. Pittsburgh tacked on a field goal in the fourth quarter to round out the upset victory.

In one of the most satisfying victories in team history, the Steelers had delivered an answer to the chanting question Cincinnati fans had posed on their trip to Pittsburgh a month earlier.

In the locker room the Steelers were thrilled and gave the ultimate payback with a familiar-sounding chant. Bill Cowher looked at his group of warriors and started screaming, "When I say Who Dey, you say We Dey. Who dey? We dey! Who dey? We Dey! Who dey think gonna beat dem Bengals?!" The answer was a resounding "We Dey!"[1]

BOXSCORE

TEAM	1st	2nd	3rd	4th	FINAL
Pittsburgh	0	14	14	3	31
Cincinnati	10	7	0	0	17

TEAM	PLAY	SCORE
Cincinnati	Graham 23-yard field goal	0–3
Cincinnati	Johnson 20-yard run (Graham kick)	0–10
Pittsburgh	Parker 19-yard pass from Roethlisberger (Reed kick)	7–10
Cincinnati	Houshmandzadeh 7-yard pass from Kitna (Graham kick)	7–17
Pittsburgh	Ward 5-yard pass from Roethlisberger (Reed kick)	14–17
Pittsburgh	Bettis 5-yard run (Reed kick)	21–17
Pittsburgh	Wilson 43-yard pass from Roethlisberger (Reed kick)	28–17
Pittsburgh	Reed 21-yard field goal	31–17

RUSHING

PITT	ATT	YDS	AVE	TD
Bettis	10	52	5.2	1
Parker	16	38	2.4	0
Haynes	3	46	15.3	0
Randle El	1	5	5.0	0
Roethlisberger	4	3	0.8	0

RUSHING

CIN	ATT	YDS	AVE	TD
Johnson	13	56	4.3	1
Kitna	4	25	6.3	0
Perry	2	3	1.5	0
Larson	1	0	0.0	0

RECEIVING

PITT	REC	YDS	AVE	TD
Wilson	3	104	34.7	1
Parker	3	41	13.7	1
Randle El	2	15	7.5	0
Miller	2	15	7.5	0
Ward	2	10	5.0	1
Haynes	1	14	14.0	0
Tuman	1	9	9.0	0

CIN	REC	YDS	AVE	TD
Perry	6	11	1.8	0
Walter	5	73	14.6	0
Johnson	4	59	14.8	0
Houshmandzadeh	4	25	6.3	1
Johnson	2	14	7.0	0
Schobel	2	11	5.5	0
Henry	1	66	66.0	0
Kelly	1	4	4.0	0

PASSING

PITT	COMP	ATT	PCT	YDS	TD	INT
Roethlisberger	14	19	73.7	208	3	0
Bettis	0	1	00.0	0	0	0
Randle El	0	1	00.0	0	0	0

CIN	COMP	ATT	PCT	YDS	TD	INT
Kitna	24	40	60.0	197	1	2
Palmer	1	1	100.0	66	0	0

An Old-Fashioned Blowout

It had been a remarkable year for the two-time defending Super Bowl champions. After dropping four of their first five games and losing starting quarterback Terry Bradshaw to injury, the Steelers ripped off nine straight victories behind a defense that allowed only 28 points during the entire streak. With Rocky Bleier and Franco Harris becoming just the second pair of teammates to both rush for over 1,000 yards in the same season, the offense found its rhythm, and Pittsburgh won the AFC Central and made the playoffs, looking to win a third consecutive Super Bowl championship. But that wouldn't come easy.

The Steelers would have to hit the road for their divisional playoff game, as they drew the tough Baltimore Colts, who'd won the AFC East with an 11–3 record. While talented, Baltimore was the antithesis of the Steelers, succeeding on the strength of a sleek offensive charge led by quarterback Bert Jones and running back Lydell Mitchell. The Colts led the league with 417 points scored in 1976 and hoped to light up the scoreboard against the Steelers' defense.

It was a brisk 36 degrees at kickoff at Baltimore's Memorial Stadium as Pittsburgh took the ball, but it didn't take long for the home crowd to feel much colder. They roared on the opening kickoff when the Baltimore special teams crushed Pittsburgh returner Ernie Pough on the return, and the Colts players mocked Pough as he writhed in pain on the ground. It was a moment that would have a lasting effect on Bradshaw, who quickly set out to exact revenge.

After their first two plays netted only two yards, the Steelers went into a new, aggressive formation, pulling out the tight end and sending in a third receiver, Frank Lewis. Lewis scorched the Baltimore secondary for a 76-yard touchdown catch to give the Steelers a 6–0 lead after just 99 seconds of play. "We may have lulled them a bit," Pittsburgh coach Chuck Noll said later. "They've seen us do nothing but run the ball. This was a new experience for them."[1]

On the Colts' first series, Pittsburgh's Mike Wagner intercepted a Jones pass, and Bradshaw connected with Lewis again, this time for 27 yards, to set up a field goal. Before many fans had found their seats, the home team trailed by nine points.

The Colts proved resilient though, driving 69 yards on their next series to pull within 9–7 on a Jones touchdown pass. But rather than swing the momentum, all the score did was postpone the Steelers' next body blow.

Theo Bell returned the ensuing kickoff 60 yards to set up a one-yard touchdown dive by bruising running back Reggie Harrison to make it 16–7. The Pittsburgh defense then took over, forcing two Baltimore punts on their next two possessions, and after future Hall of Famer Lynn Swann reeled in a 29-yard touchdown pass to push the lead to 16 points, the rout was on. Another interception set up another Pittsburgh field goal and the margin was 26–7 at the half.

The second half brought more of the same. Though Bradshaw had endured a difficult, injury-riddled season that saw him complete less than 48 percent of his passes, he was at his best in Baltimore, hitting on 14 of 18 for 264 yards. "Every time it is a big game," Colts tight end Raymond Chester said, "he always plays that way."[2]

The red-hot Bradshaw connected with Swann for another touchdown early in the fourth quarter, and the Steelers tacked on one more score when Harrison crossed the goal line for his second touchdown to make it 40–7.

Unfortunately for the Steelers, their prospects for a return to the Super Bowl took a bad turn late in the game when Franco Harris, who ran for 132 yards on the day, bruised his ribs on a hard hit. He was sent to the sideline with Bleier, who had injured his toe on the game's second play, and neither would be able to play in the AFC Championship the following week. Not surprisingly, they lost to the 13–1 Oakland Raiders, 24–7, ending their hopes of a "three-peat."

But in many ways it was amazing the Steelers got that far and remarkable that they were able to dominate a fine team such as the Colts on their own home field. The high-flying Baltimore offense was limited to a harmless 170 total yards, while the Steelers ran up what to that point was the most yards any Chuck Noll-coached team had ever produced, tallying 526.

As dominant as Pittsburgh was, the most memorable part of the contest didn't occur until after it concluded. Just moments after the game ended, a light airplane that had been flying low over the stadium crashed into the vacated upper deck as fans emptied the stadium. The pilot survived and served three months in prison. Had the game been close and/or lasted a few minutes longer, there is no telling how tragic this accident could have been.

In this case, the Steelers' domination not only extended their season and delivered one of the most impressive postseason victories in team history, but it also probably saved lives.

BOXSCORE

TEAM	1st	2nd	3rd	4th	FINAL
Pittsburgh	9	17	0	14	40
Baltimore	7	0	0	7	14

TEAM	PLAY	SCORE
Pittsburgh	Lewis 76-yard pass from Bradshaw (kick failed)	6–0
Pittsburgh	Gerela 45-yard field goal	9–0
Baltimore	Carr 17-yard pass from Jones (Linhart kick)	9–7
Pittsburgh	Harrison 1-yard run (Gerela kick)	16–7
Pittsburgh	Swann 29-yard pass from Bradshaw (Gerela kick)	23–7
Pittsburgh	Gerela 25-yard field goal	26–7
Pittsburgh	Swann 11-yard pass from Bradshaw (Gerela kick)	33–7
Baltimore	Leaks 1-yard run (Linhart kick)	33–14
Pittsburgh	Harrison 10-yard run (Gerela kick)	40–14

RUSHING

PITT	ATT	YDS	AVE	TD
Harris	18	132	7.3	0
Fuqua	11	54	4.9	0
Harrison	10	40	4.0	2

BALT	ATT	YDS	AVE	TD
Mitchell	16	55	3.4	0
Leaks	4	12	3.0	1
Jones	2	3	1.5	0
McCauley	1	1	1.0	0

RECEIVING

PITT	REC	YDS	AVE	TD
Swann	5	77	15.4	2
Harrison	4	37	9.3	0
Harris	3	24	8.0	0
Lewis	2	103	51.5	1
Fuqua	2	34	17.0	0
Bell	2	25	12.5	0
Stallworth	1	8	8.0	0

BALT	REC	YDS	AVE	TD
Mitchell	5	42	8.4	0
Chester	3	42	14.0	0
Carr	2	35	17.5	1
Doughty	1	25	25.0	0

PASSING

PITT	COMP	ATT	PCT	YDS	TD	INT
Bradshaw	14	18	77.8	264	3	0
Kruczek	5	6	83.3	44	0	0

BALT	COMP	ATT	PCT	YDS	TD	INT
Jones	11	25	44.0	144	1	2

STEELERS 20, NEW YORK JETS 17
JANUARY 15, 2005

The Kicker's Graveyard

For 30 years, Three Rivers Stadium was one of the most intimidating places to play in the NFL. It had little personality, and aesthetically there was nothing unique about it. It was a "cookie-cutter" facility built in the same mold as the several multipurpose stadiums constructed during the late 1960s and early 1970s.

After three primarily successful decades, Three Rivers became outdated, giving way to a new stadium, Heinz Field, which opened in 2001. Unlike its predecessor, Heinz Field was both unique and aesthetically pleasing, defined by several open sections in which fans inside the stadium could look out upon the city. The openness removed the din of trapped sound that had defined Three Rivers, but it inadvertently created a new type of home-field advantage. It allowed an unpredictable airflow into the stadium, particularly around the goalposts at the open end of the field. And when a timely gust of wind burst through the open section, it could change the impact of a ballgame.

The impact on the kicking game was amazing, as the successful field-goal rate was 10 percent lower at Heinz Field than across all other NFL stadiums. It quickly became a graveyard for kickers, reflected by the quick exit of Kris Brown, the first Pittsburgh kicker to try to test the unpredictable winds, and who struggled with the conditions and bolted for free agency the first chance he got.

There would be another kicker who proved to be the ultimate victim of Heinz Field's shifting air currents, and on a much grander stage.

When the New York Jets upset the San Diego Chargers in the first round of the AFC playoffs in 2004, few expected them to give the high-flying Steelers much of a game. Pittsburgh had won 14 straight and entered the postseason with a 15–1 record, plus they had defeated the Jets easily in a regular season matchup a month earlier. But the upstart Jets wound up giving the Steelers all they could handle.

Pittsburgh jumped to a 10–0 lead in the second quarter, and a rout appeared imminent. New York persevered, getting on the board with a field goal by kicker Doug Brien and then tying the game just before the half on a 75-yard punt return for a touchdown by Santana Moss.

Both offenses struggled in the second half, but late in the third period the Steelers marched into New York territory and were poised to break the tie. Then rookie quarterback Ben Roethlisberger, who'd taken the league by storm in his rookie season, threw an ill-advised pass that was intercepted by New York's Reggie Tongue at the 14. Tongue ran it back 86 yards for a touchdown to give the Jets a 17–10 lead before a stunned home crowd.

The Steelers squandered another opportunity on their next possession when Jerome Bettis—who hadn't fumbled in his last 353 carries—lost the ball after Pittsburgh drove to the New York 18. The Jets recovered, and the chances of an upset now became very real.

You don't get to be 15–1 without being able to overcome adversity, and the Steelers did just that as they tied the score on their next possession when Roethlisberger hit Hines Ward on a four-yard scoring toss with just over six minutes remaining.

Now it was the Jets who showed their toughness, moving the ball to the Pittsburgh 28 with 2:02 left. But Heinz Field collected another victim for its kicker graveyard when Brien's 45-yard attempt hit the goalpost, keeping the score knotted and giving Pittsburgh great field position.

Roethlisberger, showing an unreliability that had not been seen all season, gave the ball right back to the Jets when he threw another interception. With time running out, New York carefully drove to the Pittsburgh 24, where Brien would get a second chance to win it on the last play of regulation. No kicker had ever missed two field-goal attempts in the last two minutes of a playoff game, but none had ever faced such a challenge in Heinz Field. Incredibly, Brien's second kick was worse than his first, slicing wide left, and the Steelers' season had been saved. The game would go to overtime.

After battling through 12 nerve-racking minutes in the extra period, the Steelers finally moved deep into Jets territory to set up a game-winning field-goal attempt of their own. And kicker Jeff Reed, who already had proven far more successful at Heinz Field than any other kicker, connected on his 19th straight field goal, giving the Steelers a 20–17 win and propelling them into the AFC Championship.

Like most fans in Pittsburgh and New York, Steelers linebacker Larry Foote was dumbfounded by Brien's two misses. "I've never seen anything like it," he said. "I'm not going to say it was a miracle, because that's crippled people getting up and walking, the blind seeing. But that's the closest thing to it I've ever seen."[1]

It was no miracle. And considering Heinz Field's infamous reputation as a graveyard for kickers, perhaps it shouldn't have even been surprising.

BOXSCORE

TEAM	1st	2nd	3rd	4th	OT	FINAL
New York	0	10	7	0	0	17
Pittsburgh	10	0	0	7	3	20

TEAM	PLAY	SCORE
Pittsburgh	Reed 45-yard field goal	0–3
Pittsburgh	Bettis 3-yard run (Reed kick)	0–10
New York	Brien 42-yard kick	3–10
New York	Moss 75-yard punt return (Brien kick)	10–10
New York	Tongue 86-yard interception return (Brien kick)	17–10
Pittsburgh	Ward 4-yard pass from Roethlisberger (Reed kick)	17–17
Pittsburgh	Reed 33-yard field goal	17–20

RUSHING

PITT	ATT	YDS	AVE	TD
Bettis	27	101	3.7	1
Staley	11	54	4.9	0
Roethlisberger	4	30	7.5	0
Haynes	1	8	8.0	0

NY	ATT	YDS	AVE	TD
Martin	19	77	4.0	0
Jordan	5	30	6.0	0
Pennington	2	3	1.5	0

RECEIVING

PITT	REC	YDS	AVE	TD
Ward	10	105	10.5	1
Burress	2	28	14.0	0
Mays	2	19	9.5	0
Bettis	1	21	21.0	0
Randle El	1	6	6.0	0
Haynes	1	2	2.0	0

NY	REC	YDS	AVE	TD
McCareins	5	82	16.4	0
Moss	4	31	7.8	0
Martin	4	29	7.3	0
Sowell	3	11	3.7	0
Becht	2	15	7.5	0
Baker	2	8	4.0	0
Jordan	1	6	6.0	0

PASSING

PITT	COMP	ATT	PCT	YDS	TD	INT
Roethlisberger	17	30	56.7	181	1	2

NY	COMP	ATT	PCT	YDS	TD	INT
Pennington	21	33	63.6	182	0	1

STEELERS 24, SAN DIEGO CHARGERS 2
DECEMBER 17, 1972

Champions at Last

It wasn't what owner Art Rooney imagined when he paid $2,500 for the Pitts-burgh Steelers in 1933: in 39 years of futility and frustration, there was only one realistic shot of a championship.

Other than in 1947, when the Steelers tied for the Eastern Division crown and lost to Philadelphia in a playoff, they'd occasionally sniff first place but could never get over the hump. Finally, a quarter century after their only legitimate title opportunity, salvation arrived.

Under the direction of head coach Chuck Noll—born, ironically, in 1933—the Steelers gradually improved over his first four seasons, quietly becoming stronger through deft drafts and an attention to detail the team had lacked for decades. Noll had directed his club from oblivion to the precipice of a central division championship.

Going into the final game of the 1972 season, Pittsburgh was 10–3, having already set a team record for wins in a season. At the beginning of the day, the Steelers held a one-game lead over the Cleveland Browns, who pulled within a half game of Pittsburgh with a win over the Jets early that afternoon. The Steelers would have to defeat the 4–8–1 San Diego Chargers on the road in order to clinch their first-ever outright division crown.

From the first series, the Steelers showed they were determined to exorcise the demons of their past. On the third play of the game, safety Ralph Ander-son intercepted a San Diego pass and returned it to the San Diego 7. Three plays later, rookie running back Franco Harris, who'd already topped 1,000 yards rushing, pounded the ball into the end zone from two yards out to give Pittsburgh a 7–0 lead.

Five minutes later the Chargers responded with what proved to be their only points of the afternoon. Following a punt that trapped the Steelers deep in their own territory, Terry Bradshaw was caught in his own end zone and was sacked by defensive tackle Dave Costa for a safety that cut Pittsburgh's margin to 7–2.

A blocked Pittsburgh field goal early in the second quarter didn't halt the Steelers' momentum, and they came right back down the field and scored another touchdown on a short John Fuqua to make it 14–2 at the half.

The Steelers managed to endure through a sloppy third quarter that saw the teams combine for four turnovers, the last of which—an interception by linebacker Jack Ham—set up a Roy Gerela field goal that pushed the lead to 15 points. Moments after a 72-yard touchdown pass from Terry Bradshaw to Ron Shanklin was wiped out on a penalty, the pair connected on a 17-yard scoring strike to put the icing on the Steelers' cake, rounding out the scoring with six minutes left in the contest.

When the clock finally hit zero, Noll was carried off the field as the franchise's first championship coach. He was thrilled yet reserved after the game, letting his players celebrate their impressive moment while quietly fading into the background. "Heck, I didn't do anything to quiet them down," Noll said. "They're still yelling and I'll let them yell. It's a great win."[1]

For the team's patriarch, Art Rooney, it was as emotional a victory as he'd ever experienced. It wasn't in Rooney's nature to expose such emotions, and, appropriately, his brief postgame comments deflected all the praise to the players. "Gee, it's sure great to win," he said. "Our boys were playing with physical handicaps, but they stayed in there all day." Quiet and dignified on the outside, internally Rooney was jubilant. This was the greatest moment his team had ever experienced to that point. After 40 years, the Pittsburgh Steelers were champions at last.[2]

BOXSCORE

TEAM	1st	2nd	3rd	4th	FINAL
Pittsburgh	7	7	3	7	24
San Diego	2	0	0	0	2

TEAM	PLAY	SCORE
Pittsburgh	Harris 2-yard run (Gerela kick)	7–0
San Diego	Costa tackled Bradshaw for safety	7–2
Pittsburgh	Fuqua 2-yard run (Gerela kick)	14–2
Pittsburgh	Gerela 26-yard field goal	17–2
Pittsburgh	Shanklin 17-yard pass from Bradshaw (Gerela kick)	24–2

RUSHING

PITT	ATT	YDS	AVE	TD
Fuqua	17	51	3.0	1
Harris	15	34	2.3	1
Bradshaw	3	15	5.0	0
Pearson	2	15	7.5	0
Davis	2	0	0.0	0

SD	ATT	YDS	AVE	TD
Edwards	13	52	4.0	0
Garrett	14	5	0.4	0
Hadl	2	4	2.0	0
Clark	1	-5	-5.0	0

RECEIVING

PITT	REC	YDS	AVE	TD
Fuqua	3	50	16.7	0
Young	3	42	14.0	0
Shanklin	2	32	16.0	0
McMakin	2	12	6.0	0
Lewis	1	13	13.0	0
Harris	1	3	3.0	0

RECEIVING

SD	REC	YDS	AVE	TD
Edwards	3	42	14.0	0
Dicus	2	18	9.0	0
Garrison	2	11	5.5	0
Norman	1	24	24.0	0
Carter	1	14	14.0	0
Garrett	1	10	10.0	0
Mackey	1	3	3.0	0

PASSING

PITT	COMP	ATT	PCT	YDS	TD	INT
Bradshaw	12	23	52.2	152	1	1
Hanratty	0	1	00.0	0	0	0

SD	COMP	ATT	PCT	YDS	TD	INT
Hadl	11	26	42.3	122	0	4

#26

STEELERS 35, PHILADELPHIA EAGLES 24
OCTOBER 19, 1947

Changing of the Guard

Try as they might, the first 13 seasons that the Steelers played in the National Football League were mostly mired in mediocrity at best, as they had produced just one winning season.

Following World War II—which presented a trying time for the Steelers and the NFL as a whole—Art Rooney had hired Jock Sutherland, the former coach at the University of Pittsburgh, to lead his club. Sutherland brought some hope in 1946 with a 5–5–1 campaign, and the Steelers began the '47 season with promise, splitting their first four games before an important contest against their intrastate rivals, the Philadelphia Eagles.

The game marked a crossroad for Pittsburgh's season. With a win over perennial contender Philadelphia, the Steelers could perhaps take the first step toward title contention themselves. With a loss, the early season momentum would be lost, and they'd be well on their way to disappointing their long-suffering fans once again.

On a crisp autumn afternoon, 33,538 eager Steelers fans filed into Forbes Field to see if the Same Old Steelers would show up, or if things truly were about to change. The Steelers started strong, recovering a fumble in Philadelphia territory that set up a 39-yard touchdown reception by Tony Compagno for the game's first score.

The Eagles bounced back, though, and dominated the rest of the first half, promptly tying the game with a touchdown on their next possession and building a 10-point lead. The Steelers cut the margin to three with another touchdown set up by a 51-yard reception by Paul White, but Philadelphia scored again just before the half to make it 24–14.

The Eagles appeared to put the game away early in the third quarter with another touchdown that would have pushed the lead to 17 points, but a penalty wiped out the play, and moments later an interception by Pittsburgh's Walt Slater halted the drive and changed the game's momentum.

Pittsburgh scored early in the fourth quarter on a touchdown reception by Bill Garnass to make it 24–21, and, though they still trailed, the Steelers had taken command. After forcing a Philadelphia punt, the Steelers drove 91 yards, with several key receptions by Val Jansante. Clement capped the drive with a 23-yard scramble into the end zone to give Pittsburgh a 28–24 advantage.

Compagno promptly picked off another pass on Philadelphia's next possession, sparking another impressive drive by the Pittsburgh offense that ended on a one-yard scoring plunge by Steve Lach. It rounded out the scoring at 35–24 and capped a highly satisfying Pittsburgh victory.

Amazingly, the 35 points tied a franchise scoring record. More importantly, with the Redskins losing to the Packers that afternoon, suddenly the Steelers found themselves atop the Eastern Division standings.

Philadelphia would bounce back with a pair of 21–0 victories over the Steelers later in the season, the second of which gave the Eagles the Eastern Division title. But on this October afternoon, Pittsburgh sent a message: there truly was a changing of the guard in the NFL, and the Steelers were no longer a team that could be taken for granted.

BOXSCORE

TEAM	1st	2nd	3rd	4th	FINAL
Philadelphia	10	14	0	0	24
Pittsburgh	7	7	0	21	35

TEAM	PLAY	SCORE
Pittsburgh	Compagno 29-yard pass from Clement (Glamp kick)	0–7
Philadelphia	Pihos 43-yard pass from Thompson (Patton kick)	7–7
Philadelphia	Patton 14-yard field goal	10–7
Philadelphia	Pritchard 69-yard pass from Thompson (Patton kick)	17–7
Pittsburgh	Clement 5-yard run (Glamp kick)	17–14
Philadelphia	Pihos 17-yard pass from Thompson (Patton kick)	24–14
Pittsburgh	Garnass 19-yard pass from Clement (Glamp kick)	24–21
Pittsburgh	Clement 23-yard run (Glamp kick)	24–28
Pittsburgh	Lach 1-yard run (Glamp kick)	24–35

STEELERS 34, NEW ENGLAND PATRIOTS 20
OCTOBER 31, 2004

Streak Breakers

Perfection is what great teams aspire to. It's not enough to capture division titles or Super Bowl championships; they want to dominate teams every time they take the field. They want to be remembered as the greatest that ever took the gridiron. The 2004 New England Patriots were such a team.

Fresh off their second Super Bowl championship in three years, the Patriots were now working on establishing themselves as one of the best teams ever. Not just for their Super Bowl titles, but for an unprecedented winning streak that they brought into their Week Seven encounter with the Steelers at Heinz Field.

Since losing to the Washington Redskins on September 28, 2003, the Patriots hadn't lost a single game. They'd won the final 12 games of the 2003 season, swept through a trio of postseason games, and then won their first six contests of 2004 to extend the string to 18 consecutive victories, 21 including the postseason. It was a new record, the longest winning streak in NFL history.

Looking to etch their names in history as the team that snapped the streak, the Steelers got off to a surprisingly good start in 2004 themselves. With rookie Ben Roethlisberger settling into his new role as starting quarterback, Pittsburgh had won five straight, the longest streak ever for a rookie starting quarterback. With a pair of historic streaks meeting head-on, something had to give.

New England was without starting running back Corey Dillon, who had injured his thigh, but early on it looked like they wouldn't miss him. The Patriots marched down the field on their first possession and took an early 3–0 lead as Adam Vinatieri connected on a 43-yard field goal.

A year earlier, that likely would have been enough to convince the Steelers they were in over their heads. But Ben Roethlisberger was no ordinary rookie and had transcended the Steelers into something better. Recognizing that New

England All-Pro cornerback Ty Law was out with an injury, Roethlisberger focused on wideout Plaxico Burress. He hit Burress for a diving 47-yard touchdown reception that gave the Steelers a lead they wouldn't relinquish and began a long day for Law's replacement, Randall Gay. "He was a lame duck out there," Burress said, "so we just went right at him."[1]

On New England's next possession, Pittsburgh linebacker Joey Porter sacked Patriots star quarterback Tom Brady, forcing a fumble that the Steelers recovered to set up another Roethlisberger-to-Burress touchdown toss that made it 14–3. And Pittsburgh wasn't done. As the first quarter came to an end, Steelers defensive back Deshea Townsend intercepted a Brady pass and returned it 39 yards for a touchdown and a 21–3 Pittsburgh lead. The Heinz Field crowd roared, nearly delirious with surprise.

With Big Ben looking like the wily veteran and Brady the untested rookie, things continued on a downward spiral for New England in the second quarter. Another Brady interception set up a Pittsburgh field goal before the Patriots finally got into the end zone to stop the bleeding late in the first half.

Though the Steelers had dominated and led by two touchdowns, the deficit wasn't insurmountable for a team like the Patriots. The Steelers needed a knockout punch, and early in the third quarter, they landed it.

Another crushing Porter hit forced another fumble, which the Steelers' Aaron Smith recovered and returned to the New England 17. Jerome Bettis took it from there, pounding into the end zone four plays later to make it 31–10, Pittsburgh. It was a touchdown that for all intents and purposes put the stake in the heart of the Patriots record-setting streak.

The teams exchanged field goals, and Brady did throw a meaningless touchdown pass midway in the fourth quarter, but the Steelers continued to dominate the line of scrimmage. Bettis continually barreled through the New England defensive line and ate up the final 6:27 of the game, closing out Pittsburgh's convincing 34–20 victory.

The Steelers dominated the game statistically, outgaining New England in total yardage, 417 to 248. New England Head Coach Bill Belichick, not used to seeing his team pushed around like that, was dumbfounded. "It was pretty obvious the Steelers were the better team," he said. "They outcoached us, outplayed us, and we weren't good in any phase of the game. We didn't do much of anything right."[2]

It was a momentary lapse for the champions, as they won 11 of their last 12 games, including a 41–27 victory against the Steelers in the AFC Championship, and then defending their Super Bowl championship against the Eagles two weeks later. On this day, though, they were anything but perfect as Pittsburgh was nothing short of great themselves, taking their role of streak breakers very seriously.

BOXSCORE

TEAM	1st	2nd	3rd	4th	FINAL
New England	3	7	3	7	20
Pittsburgh	21	3	10	0	34

TEAM	PLAY	SCORE
New England	Vinatieri 43-yard field goal	3–0
Pittsburgh	Burress 47-yard pass from Roethlisberger (Reed kick)	3–7
Pittsburgh	Burress 4-yard pass from Roethlisberger (Reed kick)	3–14
Pittsburgh	Townsend 39-yard interception return (Reed kick)	3–21
Pittsburgh	Reed 19-yard field goal	3–24
New England	Givens 2-yard pass from Brady (Vinatieri kick)	10–24
Pittsburgh	Bettis 2-yard run (Reed kick)	10–31
New England	Vinatieri 25-yard field goal	13–31
Pittsburgh	Reed 29-yard field goal	13–34
New England	Givens 23-yard pass from Brady (Vinatieri kick)	20–34

RUSHING

PITT	ATT	YDS	AVE	TD
Staley	25	125	5.0	0
Bettis	15	65	4.3	1
Haynes	3	17	5.7	0
Ward	1	11	11.0	0
Roethlisberger	5	3	0.6	0

RUSHING

NE	ATT	YDS	AVE	TD
Faulk	5	4	0.8	0
Cobbs	1	1	1.0	0

RECEIVING

PITT	REC	YDS	AVE	TD
Ward	6	58	9.7	0
Randle El	6	44	7.3	0
Burress	3	63	21.0	2
Haynes	2	18	9.0	0
Kreider	1	13	13.0	0

NE	REC	YDS	AVE	TD
Givens	8	101	12.6	2
Faulk	8	72	9.0	0
Brown	5	59	11.8	0
Patten	4	39	9.8	0

PASSING

PITT	COMP	ATT	PCT	YDS	TD	INT
Roethlisberger	18	24	75.0	196	2	0

NE	COMP	ATT	PCT	YDS	TD	INT
Brady	25	43	58.1	271	2	2

STEELERS 34, HOUSTON OILERS 5
JANUARY 7, 1979

A Quagmire on Turf

In the late 1970s, the Houston Oilers were among the best teams in the National Football League. With a productive offense, a stonewall defense, and a coaching staff that knew how to get the best out of players, the Oilers were solid all around and respected across the league. There was only one thing that prevented Houston from grabbing the Lombardi Trophy—a bitter division rival donned in black and gold.

The Oilers' potential dynasty ran into timing issues. As they hit their peak in the mid- and late 1970s, the Pittsburgh Steelers were without a doubt the team of the decade. Even Houston coach Bum Phillips realized his team's dilemma, often repeating what became a trademark phrase: "The road to the Super Bowl runs through Pittsburgh." And the Steelers' dynasty may have peaked in 1978, when they put together what is often remembered as one of the greatest teams of all time. Thus, in the 1978 AFC Championship, the Oilers' road to the Super Bowl not only ran through Pittsburgh but also was thoroughly covered with ice.

The cold was a big enough obstacle for a warm-weather team that played in a climate-controlled stadium, but on this frosty January day, a horrific ice storm hit the Steel City. The rain started falling before the game as the temperatures began to fall. Roads around Three Rivers Stadium were a sheet of ice as were the sidewalks and steps coming down from the bridge where the sellout throng was walking toward the stadium. What was normally a 15-minute walk from downtown to Three Rivers, where many of the patrons would park, was taking upwards of an hour.

Throughout the previous week, the Oilers appeared confident. Defensive end Elvin Bethea went so far as to guarantee a victory. But the combination of the foul weather and a Pittsburgh team determined to become the first in the NFL to win three Super Bowls provided a formidable challenge for the Houston Oilers, who looked outmatched from the outset.

Even with Terry Bradshaw battling the flu, the Steelers quickly drove downfield on their first possession, taking a quick 7–0 lead on a Franco Harris touchdown run. A Houston turnover led to a Rocky Bleier touchdown, putting the Steelers up 14–0 going into the second quarter.

In the opening moments of the second period, the Steelers landed another haymaker when safety Mike Wagner blasted Houston tight end Mike Barber, knocking Barber out of the game. But as physical as the Steelers were, the story of the first half was both teams' inability to hold onto the football amidst the icy conditions. By halftime, they had tied an NFL playoff record with 10 combined fumbles and then set the mark with two more. This propensity for fumbling doomed the Oilers just before the intermission.

After the Oilers had cut the lead to 14–3, they had a chance to claw back into the game after a 15-yard completion from quarterback Dan Pastorini to receiver Ronny Coleman moved them to the Pittsburgh 30. But before Coleman was down, Steelers linebacker Jack Ham stripped the ball and recovered the fumble, ending the Houston threat. Then, with just 52 seconds left in the half, Bradshaw hit Lynn Swann for a 29-yard scoring strike to make it 21–3. But Houston wasn't done handing Pittsburgh scoring opportunities.

On the ensuing kickoff, Houston's Johnnie Dirden fumbled back to the Steelers on the Houston 17, and Bradshaw found John Stallworth in the end zone for another touchdown and a whopping 25-point lead. Amazingly, the lead swelled even larger moments later when Coleman fumbled the ball for the second time in the last 90 seconds of the half. This one led to a 37-yard Roy Gerela field goal with four seconds left to extend the Steeler advantage to 31–3.

Twenty-nine minutes of relatively solid Oilers football had been obliterated in less than 60 seconds. With the weather worsening, the 17 points Pittsburgh put up in the final minute of the half rendered the game essentially over, with the last 30 minutes being nothing more than a victory lap.

A short Steelers field goal and a Houston safety in the third quarter were the only points the teams could muster in the second half, and Houston's quest to dethrone the champions turned out to be an exercise in icy futility.

Bum Phillips's club had been soundly defeated, but Houston's coach was dignified afterward, visiting the Steelers' locker room and offering the team his congratulations. "You've got a helluva a team," he said to Pittsburgh center Mike Webster. "You can be proud of it. Believe me, I'm proud of the way you fellows played football."[1]

Phillips's quarterback also offered no excuses. "We simply lost to a better team," Pastorini said. "Purely and simply, they whipped us."[2]

The weather took its toll, especially on the already-ill Bradshaw, who was chilled to the point of trembling until he warmed up in the team's sauna. But while Bradshaw warmed up and would recover in time to lead the team into the Super Bowl two weeks later, the Oilers took their cold disappointment into the offseason, knowing they'd fallen short to perhaps the only team in the NFL tougher than themselves.

BOXSCORE

TEAM	1st	2nd	3rd	4th	FINAL
Houston	0	3	2	0	5
Pittsburgh	14	17	3	0	34

TEAM	PLAY	SCORE
Pittsburgh	Harris 7-yard run (Gerela kick)	0–7
Pittsburgh	Bleier 15-yard run (Gerela kick)	0–14
Houston	Fritsch 19-yard field goal	3–14
Pittsburgh	Swann 29-yard pass from Bradshaw (Gerela kick)	3–21
Pittsburgh	Stallworth 17-yard pass from Bradshaw (Gerela kick)	3–28
Pittsburgh	Gerela 37-yard field goal	3–31
Pittsburgh	Gerela 22-yard field goal	3–34
Houston	Washington tackled Bleier in the end zone	5–34

RUSHING

PITT	ATT	YDS	AVE	TD
Harris	20	51	2.7	1
Bleier	10	45	4.5	1
Bradshaw	7	29	4.2	0
Deloplaine	3	28	9.3	0
Thornton	3	22	7.3	0
Moser	3	7	2.3	0
Kruczek	1	-3	-3.0	0

RUSHING

HOU	ATT	YDS	AVE	TD
Campbell	22	62	2.8	0
Woods	1	9	9.0	0
Wilson	2	6	3.0	0
Coleman	1	-5	-5.0	0

RECEIVING

PITT	REC	YDS	AVE	TD
Swann	4	98	24.5	1
Bleier	4	42	10.5	0
Grossman	2	43	21.5	0
Stallworth	1	17	17.0	0

HOU	REC	YDS	AVE	TD
Caster	5	44	8.8	0
Wilson	5	33	6.6	0
Coleman	1	15	15.0	0
Campbell	1	4	4.0	0

PASSING

PITT	COMP	ATT	PCT	YDS	TD	INT
Bradshaw	11	19	57.9	200	2	2

HOU	COMP	ATT	PCT	YDS	TD	INT
Pastorini	12	26	46.2	96	0	5

#23

STEELERS 34, DENVER BRONCOS 17
JANUARY 22, 2006

Road Warriors

AFC title games had not been kind to Bill Cowher. By 2005, while he'd enjoyed a wonderful 14-year career as head coach of his hometown team, getting his club to five AFC Championship games, he had been successful in only one. That had been in 1995 against the heavy underdog Indianapolis Colts, and even that had gone down to the wire. Interestingly, all five had been played in Pittsburgh, and the Steelers had been favored each time. Cowher seemed snakebit. He was one of the most successful coaches of his time, yet he still struggled to get over the hump of the conference title game.

The Steelers' sixth venture into the AFC Championship in the Cowher era had a different feel to it. Not only would the Steelers be the road team against the second-seeded Denver Broncos, but they'd taken a highly unlikely path to the Super Bowl's doorstep. Making the playoffs as a wild card, the Steelers had upset division rival Bengals in Cincinnati in the first round and then stunned No. 1 seed Indianapolis on the road in a divisional playoff. Not surprisingly, this time around, the Steelers were not the favorite to represent the AFC in the Super Bowl.

Cowher had embraced the underdog role throughout the playoff run, and his players were inspired by the idea that no one had given them a chance to get to the Super Bowl. Longtime Pittsburgh radio announcer Bill Hillgrove dubbed the team the "Road Warriors," and the name fit, but never more than on this sunshiny afternoon in the Rocky Mountains.

The Broncos, who'd defeated the Steelers in Pittsburgh in the AFC title game eight years earlier, came into this title clash undefeated for the season at Denver's Invesco Field. Led by former Arizona State quarterback Jake Plummer and a pair of talented running backs, Mike Anderson and Tatum Bell, the

Denver offense was both well balanced and explosive. Conversely, Denver's defense was its Achilles' heel, ranked 29th in the league in defending the pass.

Cowher attacked this weakness from the outset, unleashing his second-year quarterback Ben Roethlisberger. On the Steelers' first drive of the game, Roethlisberger completed five passes for 53 yards and led Pittsburgh downfield for a 47-yard Jeff Reed field goal. On the ensuing Broncos possession, linebacker Joey Porter sacked Plummer, forcing a fumble that nose tackle Casey Hampton pounced on at the Denver 39. Roethlisberger picked up where he left off, hitting Heath Miller for 24 yards and then Cedrick Wilson for a 12-yard touchdown pass as Pittsburgh quickly took a surprising 10–0 lead in the opening seconds of the second quarter.

The Broncos trimmed the lead to seven points with a field goal of their own, but then Roethlisberger got rolling once again. Five more completions combined with a few powerful running plays jammed the ball down the Broncos' throats during a 14-play, seven-minute drive. It ended with a Jerome Bettis three-yard run into the end zone for a 17–3 lead with only two minutes left in the half.

Making matters worse for the home team, Pittsburgh's Ike Taylor intercepted a Plummer pass moments later. And after a quick and effective Steelers drive, the lead stretched to 24–3 when Hines Ward caught a 17-yard touchdown pass just before the half. The home fans, expecting to see their Broncos cruise to victory over the upstart Steelers, were stunned.

The Broncos fought back in the second half, cutting the margin to 10 points midway through the fourth quarter, as the Pittsburgh offense was unable to keep up its red-hot first-half pace. After another defensive stop, Denver regained possession at its own 20 with six minutes remaining with momentum on its side. But on a critical third-down play moments later, Pittsburgh's Brett Keisel sacked Plummer and stripped the football. Travis Kirschke pounced on the football to halt Denver's surge and all but sew up Pittsburgh's sixth AFC title.

Jerome Bettis, who had returned for a 13th season for the opportunity to finally win the Super Bowl that eluded him for his entire career, put the icing on the cake. He pounded the ball to the Denver four-yard line, where Roethlisberger ran it in for the Steelers' fourth touchdown.

In one afternoon, they'd accomplished everything they'd been unable to do in their previous AFC Championship appearances under Bill Cowher: completely dominate the game from beginning to end. Not surprisingly, the coach was emotional afterward. "This is a great group of guys," he said. "We're a different team. We're a focused team, and no matter what's happened, we've stayed together. We've got a resilient group."[1]

It was indeed. By pulling off a feat they'd never been able to achieve at home, this team truly earned the label of Road Warriors.

BOXSCORE

TEAM	1st	2nd	3rd	4th	FINAL
Pittsburgh	3	21	0	10	34
Denver	0	3	7	7	17

TEAM	PLAY	SCORE
Pittsburgh	Reed 47-yard field goal	3–0
Pittsburgh	Wilson 12-yard pass from Roethlisberger (Reed kick)	10–0
Denver	Elam 23-yard field goal	10–3
Pittsburgh	Bettis 3-yard run (Reed kick)	17–3
Pittsburgh	Ward 17-yard pass from Roethlisberger (Reed kick)	24–3
Denver	Lelie 30-yard pass from Plummer (Elam kick)	24–10
Pittsburgh	Reed 42-yard field goal	27–10
Denver	Anderson 3-yard run (Elam kick)	27–17
Pittsburgh	Roethlisberger 4-yard run (Reed kick)	34–17

RUSHING

PITT	ATT	YDS	AVE	TD
Bettis	15	39	2.6	1
Parker	14	35	2.5	0
Roethlisberger	3	12	4.0	1
Ward	1	4	4.0	0

DEN	ATT	YDS	AVE	TD
Anderson	9	36	4.0	1
Bell	5	31	6.2	0
Plummer	7	30	4.3	0

RECEIVING

PITT	REC	YDS	AVE	TD
Wilson	5	92	18.4	1
Ward	5	59	11.8	1
Randle El	4	52	13.0	0
Parker	3	20	6.7	0
Miller	2	31	15.5	0
Washington	1	13	13.0	0
Haynes	1	8	8.0	0

DEN	REC	YDS	AVE	TD
Bell	5	28	5.6	0
Smith	4	61	15.3	0
Putzier	4	55	13.8	0
Anderson	3	11	3.7	0
Lelie	2	68	34.0	1

PASSING

PITT	COMP	ATT	PCT	YDS	TD	INT
Roethlisberger	21	29	72.4	275	2	0

DEN	COMP	ATT	PCT	YDS	TD	INT
Plummer	18	30	60.0	223	1	2

#22

STEELERS 20, SAN FRANCISCO 49ERS 17
OCTOBER 14, 1984

The Lone Blemish

It is the most difficult feat an NFL team can achieve: a perfect season. By 1984, only seven NFL teams had run the table in the regular season, with only the 1972 Miami Dolphins carrying perfection to the league championship.

In 1984, the San Francisco 49ers were in the middle of one of the most impressive dynasties the league had ever seen, and this season was shaping into the most dominant of the era. Joe Montana was now one of the top three quarterbacks in the league, and Wendell Tyler gave the 49ers an effective ground game, while an unassuming defense surrendered fewer points than any other team in the league.

Week after week, they carved up opponents, marching through the post-season and to a romp of the Miami Dolphins in Super Bowl XIX. It was as close to a perfect season as you could get without technically being perfect. And it would have been, were it not for one blemish suffered on an October Sunday afternoon at Candlestick Park against the team that had produced the league's last great dynasty.

By the mid-1980s, the Steelers were a shadow of their dominant 1970s selves, with most of their Hall of Fame talent out of football. In their first year without Terry Bradshaw, they were struggling with mediocre David Woodley, who had been mostly unimpressive in Pittsburgh's 3–3 start. He'd suffered a concussion during a Week Six blowout defeat in Miami, and head coach Chuck Noll decided to start backup Mark Malone, the Steelers' first-round pick in 1980, who was supposed to have been the heir apparent to Terry Bradshaw. Instead, he'd failed to make an impression in four years backing up the aging Bradshaw and couldn't beat out Woodley once Bradshaw retired. But Malone would get a chance on this autumn afternoon by the bay.

Not only were the Steelers coming into this game with a new starting quarterback, but their offensive line was in tatters. Terry Long and Larry Brown were injured, as was tight end Chris Kolodziejski. The makeshift offensive line saw Emil Boures, Blake Wingle, Steve August, and Tunch Ilkin surrounding Hall of Fame center Mike Webster. It got so bad that Ray Snell, who was playing on a bad ankle, moved to tackle so Ilkin could play tight end, replacing Kolodziejski. It looked like a recipe for disaster, but somehow, it worked like a charm against the 6–0 49ers.

On the game's first possession, behind Webster's leadership, the tattered Steelers' front wall blew San Francisco off the line. "Webbie is great in situations like that," Ilkin said later. "He was telling the guys 'Come off the ball. Don't make mistakes. We'll get it in.'"[1]

That they did, setting the tone on the first drive, as a Pittsburgh running game that hadn't been much of a factor in the first six games powered the offense downfield and provided a 7–0 lead on a short-scoring run by Rich Erenberg.

The advantage stretched to 10–0 in the second quarter before the heralded San Francisco offense got untracked and narrowed the margin to 10–7 on a seven-yard touchdown scramble by Montana. The 49ers carried their momentum into the second half and took command, sprinting to a 17–10 lead in the fourth quarter, and it appeared their seventh consecutive victory was in the bag. But then a handful of leftovers from the Steelers' dynasty found a chink in the armor of the new kids on the block.

Webster sparked a resurgent offensive line, and the Steelers put together a long drive midway through the final period, once again on the strength of their running game. "We've always felt like we could run the ball," Ilkin said. "We just have to stick with it a little more than we have been."[2]

Stick with it they did as tailback Frank Pollard, who finished the game with 105 yards, carried the ball to the San Francisco 6 with just over three minutes left in the game. Veteran wide receiver John Stallworth, one of the stalwarts of the Steel Curtain teams, spoke up in the huddle and convinced Malone to call a play that seemed like a questionable choice. It would have Stallworth run a pattern against Ronnie Lott, one of the best defensive backs the game has ever known. Granted, Lott was hindered somewhat by an ankle injury, but Ilkin, like many of his teammates, wondered why they'd target such a player with the game on the line. "As I'm coming to the line," Ilkin said, "I was thinking to myself, 'What the heck are we doing here?'" But like magic, it worked. Stallworth, a future Hall of Famer himself, slipped behind Lott and caught the game-tying touchdown with only 3:21 left.[3]

Still, there was plenty of time left for Montana to work magic of his own to deliver another 49ers victory. But before San Francisco could reach midfield,

Pittsburgh linebacker Bryan Hinkle stepped in front of a Montana pass for an interception and then returned it 43 yards deep into San Francisco territory. It set up the go-ahead field goal with just over 90 seconds to play, and Candlestick Park became eerily silent.

This was one of the great teams in the history of the game, and the 49ers were not done. Montana shook off his mistake and drove his offense to the Pittsburgh 20 with 10 seconds left. San Francisco head coach Bill Walsh called on dependable kicker Ray Wersching to attempt a game-tying field goal that would send the game to overtime. Incredibly, Wersching's kick sailed wide, and the Steelers ran out the final seconds to secure the biggest upset of the NFL season.

Not surprisingly, Noll was impressed with his team's effort. "Super Bowl victories are great," he said. "But I don't think I've ever been associated with a victory any better than this." It was a win that was both memorable and historic. It turned out to be the only thing that kept the 1984 49ers from joining the 1972 Dolphins, while reminding Pittsburgh fans of the good old days of a bygone era—when their team was the dominant force in football.[4]

BOXSCORE

TEAM	1st	2nd	3rd	4th	FINAL
Pittsburgh	7	3	0	10	20
San Francisco	0	7	0	10	17

TEAM	PLAY	SCORE
Pittsburgh	Erenberg 2-yard run (Anderson kick)	7–0
Pittsburgh	Anderson 48-yard field goal	10–0
San Francisco	Montana 7-yard run (Wersching kick)	10–7
San Francisco	Wersching 30-yard field goal	10–10
San Francisco	Tyler 7-yard run (Wersching kick)	10–17
Pittsburgh	Stallworth 6-yard pass from Malone (Anderson kick)	17–17
Pittsburgh	Anderson 21-yard field goal	20–17

RUSHING

PITT	ATT	YDS	AVE	TD
Pollard	24	105	4.4	0
Erenberg	11	44	4.0	1
Abercrombie	8	23	2.9	0
Malone	3	2	0.7	0

SF	ATT	YDS	AVE	TD
Tyler	11	59	5.4	1
Craig	6	29	4.8	0
Montana	3	29	9.7	1

RECEIVING

PITT	REC	YDS	AVE	TD
Stallworth	6	78	13.0	1
Thompson	1	23	23.0	0
Kolodziejski	1	22	22.0	0
Erenberg	1	12	12.0	0
Capers	1	11	11.0	0
Garity	1	10	10.0	0

SF	REC	YDS	AVE	TD
Craig	7	43	6.1	0
Cooper	6	50	8.3	0
Clark	5	67	13.4	0
Francis	2	50	25.0	0
Tyler	2	13	6.5	0
Wilson	1	14	14.0	0
Monroe	1	4	4.0	0

PASSING

PITT	COMP	ATT	PCT	YDS	TD	INT
Malone	11	18	61.1	156	1	1

SF	COMP	ATT	PCT	YDS	TD	INT
Montana	24	34	70.6	241	0	1
Harmon	0	1	00.0	0	0	0

STEELERS 26, HOUSTON OILERS 23
DECEMBER 31, 1989

The Fifty-Yard Miracle

Without even taking into account what was to come, the 1989 Pittsburgh Steelers considered it a miracle just to be still playing on New Year's Eve. Seven days after the regular season ended, the Steelers were still alive—a truly remarkable achievement considering that two games into the season, they appeared decidedly dead.

In the opener against their bitter rivals from Cleveland, they suffered one of the most humiliating defeats in the history of the franchise—a 51–0 massacre on their home turf. Things didn't get much better the following week in Cincinnati when the Bengals also thrashed Pittsburgh by a count of 41–10. Two games, two horrific defeats seemed to extinguish any optimism for the 1989 season that the Steelers might make a return to the playoffs after a four-year absence, the longest in the 20-year tenure of head coach Chuck Noll.

But something happened on the way to disaster. Noll found a way to turn things around, and his young team won nine of its last 14 games to sneak into the postseason. Led by a suddenly tough defense headed by Rod Woodson and an offense run by previously embattled quarterback Bubby Brister, the Steelers would face division rival Houston in the Astrodome in the AFC Wild Card Game on the final day of the calendar year.

The Oilers had swept the season series from Pittsburgh and had been in the driver's seat to win the AFC Central before losing their final two games and backing into the playoffs as a wild card team. Houston was without a doubt the more talented team and a prohibitive favorite, but while there were many superstars dotting the rosters of each team, it would be one of the smallest men on the field that would carry the biggest weight in the classic contest, Pittsburgh kicker Gary Anderson.

The underdog Steelers let the Oilers know early on that this would not be an easy game. Pittsburgh's rookie linebacker Jerry Olsavky blocked a punt at the Oilers' 32, and the Steelers drove to the Houston 9 before the drive stalled. Rather than go for the field goal, Noll made an uncharacteristically bold decision to go for it, and rookie fullback Tim Worley took the fourth-and-one pitch through the Houston defense for a touchdown and a 7–0 Pittsburgh lead.

The teams traded field goals for the next two periods, as the Steelers held a 10–6 advantage at the intermission and then stretched the margin to 16–9 early in the fourth. The margin was narrow, but the pressure was clearly on the Oilers, whose high-powered offense had yet to reach the end zone.

For three quarters, the Pittsburgh defense held All-Pro Houston quarterback Warren Moon at bay, but Moon came alive in the fourth. He led the Oilers on an 80-yard march and tied the game with an 11-yard pass to Ernest Givins with just over nine minutes left in the game. After the Oilers' defense stuffed the Pittsburgh offense on the ensuing possession, Steelers punter Harry Newsome shanked his kick, sending it only 25 yards, and Houston took over at the Pittsburgh 38. The momentum had clearly shifted.

Things only got worse for the Steelers when Givins reeled in a 30-yard pass and then put the home team ahead with his second touchdown in three minutes to make it 23–16 with six minutes remaining.

With the Astrodome rocking, Pittsburgh's magic-carpet ride appeared at an end. With one more defensive stop, the Oilers could put the nail in the Steelers' coffin. Brister & Co. took over at their own 18 and immediately got rolling. Louis Lipps caught a 10-yard pass, and Worley ran twice for 18 more yards. Pittsburgh then surprised the Oilers with a reverse to speedy Dwight Stone, who broke loose for 22 yards to the Houston 29. With the home crowd getting quieter with each Steelers first down, the Steelers gradually pushed inside the 10 when running back Merril Hoge—who was having a tremendous game—barreled up the middle for seven yards to the Houston 2. On the next play he capped the Steelers' stunning drive by bolting into the end zone for the game-tying touchdown. Noll was impressed with the clutch drive. "It was a very emotional thing for this team," he said. "It was a gut check."[1]

If the game-tying drive was a gut check, the Steelers ended Houston's first possession in overtime with an uppercut. On a sweep around the left side, Oilers running back Lorenzo White was clobbered by both Rod Woodson and Tim Johnson and fumbled the football. Woodson picked up the ball and returned it to the Houston 46, and suddenly the Steelers had victory in their grasp. Hoge powered up the middle twice to push Pittsburgh to the Houston 33, and the time had come for Gary Anderson to carve out his space in Steelers history.

Though he'd been a very successful kicker for most of the decade, Anderson took the field knowing he hadn't attempted a field goal this long all season. "I'd be lying if I said I was totally calm out there when they called the time out," he admitted after the game. "But Tunch came over and said, 'I wouldn't want anyone out here kicking this but you,' and my teammates gave me a boost."[2]

On the ensuing play, he then returned the favor, drilling the kick through the uprights and delivering one of the most shocking upsets in the history of the franchise.

It was a fittingly stunning way to end one of the most unusual yet satisfying seasons the Pittsburgh Steelers had ever experienced. Considering they were 5–11 the year before, had kept 12 rookies on the roster, and suffered two disastrous games early in the season, they defied the odds and amazingly qualified for the playoffs on the last Sunday of the season. Despite all the incredible things that happened during the campaign, they paled in comparison to this moment, the 50-yard miracle that gave the Steelers this most dramatic victory.

BOXSCORE

TEAM	1st	2nd	3rd	4th	OT	FINAL
Pittsburgh	7	3	3	10	3	26
Houston	0	6	3	14	0	23

TEAM	PLAY	SCORE
Pittsburgh	Worley 9-yard run (Anderson kick)	7–0
Houston	Zendejas 26-yard field goal	7–3
Houston	Zendejas 35-yard field goal	7–6
Pittsburgh	Anderson 25-yard field goal	10–6
Houston	Zendejas 26-yard field goal	10–9
Pittsburgh	Anderson 30-yard field goal	13–9
Pittsburgh	Anderson 48-yard field goal	16–9
Houston	Givens 18-yard pass from Moon (Zendejas kick)	16–16
Houston	Givens 9-yard pass from Moon (Zendejas kick)	16–23
Pittsburgh	Hoge 2-yard run (Anderson kick)	23–23
Pittsburgh	Anderson 50-yard field goal	26–23

RUSHING

PITT	ATT	YDS	AVE	TD
Hoge	17	100	5.9	1
Worley	11	54	4.9	1
Stone	1	22	22.0	0
Brister	1	1	1.0	0

HOU	ATT	YDS	AVE	TD
Pinkett	8	26	3.3	0
White	7	13	1.9	0
Rozier	5	12	2.4	0
Moon	3	12	4.0	0
Highsmith	2	2	1.0	0

RECEIVING

PITT	REC	YDS	AVE	TD
Worley	4	23	5.8	0
Mularkey	3	40	13.3	0
Hoge	3	26	8.7	0
Lips	3	24	8.0	0
Hill	1	7	7.0	0
Stock	1	7	7.0	0

HOU	REC	YDS	AVE	TD
Givens	11	136	12.4	2
Hill	6	98	16.3	0
Pinkett	3	24	8.0	0
Highsmith	3	21	7.0	0
Jeffries	3	16	5.3	0
Duncan	2	15	7.5	0
Rozier	1	5	5.0	0

PASSING

PITT	COMP	ATT	PCT	YDS	TD	INT
Brister	15	33	45.5	127	0	0

HOU	COMP	ATT	PCT	YDS	TD	INT
Moon	29	48	60.4	315	2	0

STEELERS 31, BALTIMORE RAVENS 24
JANUARY 15, 2011

From the Jaws of Defeat

It didn't take long for the Steelers and Ravens to become one of the premier NFL rivalries. The once-bitter series with the rival Cleveland Browns shifted to Baltimore along with the original Browns in 1996, and by the dawn of the 21st century, Steelers fans would circle the two dates with the Ravens each season. In 2010, rabid fans of both teams had to circle one more date when the Steelers and Ravens met at Heinz Field in an AFC divisional playoff.

It would be the third time the teams had met in the postseason, with the Steelers winning the previous two in 2001 and 2008. This game would be a chance for the Ravens to gain some measure of revenge against the team that had twice ended their season in the playoffs and more recently beat them out to capture the AFC North Division title. Interestingly, while the teams split their regular season series in 2010, they each won on the opponent's home field.

While Baltimore didn't get the off week that the Steelers earned with the division crown, the Ravens tuned up by crushing the Kansas City Chiefs in a lopsided first-round matchup. Following a season in which they were plagued by injuries, the Steelers could certainly use the week of rest before facing the hungry Ravens. But even when shorthanded, the Steelers endured, exemplified by the play of Charlie Batch and Dennis Dixon in place of Ben Roethlisberger as he served a four-game suspension following a sexual assault charge. Even with their starting quarterback out, the Steelers sprinted to a 3–1 start that set the tone for the rest of the season.

Early on in the third Steelers-Ravens war of the season, it looked like the momentum Baltimore acquired the week before had carried over.

After the Steelers took an early 7–0 lead when Rashard Mendenhall's one-yard TD romp ended an 11-play, 80-yard drive, the hometown team hit the wall. Baltimore came right back to tie it on a Ray Rice 14-yard scamper and then turned to its defense to take control of the contest.

On the second play after the kickoff, Baltimore linebacker Terrell Suggs hit Roethlisberger, who lost the ball in what appeared to be an incomplete pass. As Suggs celebrated, everyone stayed almost motionless until Baltimore's Cory Redding realized that no official had blown a whistle. Redding picked up the ball and ran it the remaining 13 yards for a Baltimore touchdown. A replay review verified that Roethlisberger had indeed lost the ball before his arm came forward, and the touchdown stood.

Things were quiet until midway in the second quarter when another Steelers turnover set up more Baltimore points. A Steelers fumble at their own 16 put the Ravens in prime scoring position, and six plays later tight end Todd Heap snared a four-yard Joe Flacco pass to put the visitors up 21–7. The Steelers quickly drove downfield as the final seconds of the first half ticked down, but Shaun Suisham missed a 43-yard field goal, and the Ravens' lead remained 14 points at the intermission.

The lead was not insurmountable, but the Steelers knew this was no way to win a postseason game. "A lot of times in that situation," Hines Ward would say later, "especially in the playoffs, when you turn the ball over the way we did, a lot of teams usually give up and it ends up being a blowout." But this one would not.[1]

Early in the third quarter, Pittsburgh safety Ryan Clark forced a fumble by stripping the football from the usually sure-handed Rice to set up a nine-yard touchdown catch by Heath Miller. Six minutes later, a Pittsburgh interception led to a Roethlisberger-to-Ward eight-yard scoring pass to tie the game, and shortly after that, another Baltimore fumble led to the go-ahead field goal and a 24–21 Steelers lead.

With Pittsburgh's defense now suffocating the Baltimore offense, the Ravens' special teams provided a spark when Ladarius Webb returned a punt 55 yards to set up a tying field goal in what was quickly becoming a classic game.

With just over two minutes left and the Steelers facing third and 19 at their own 38, it appeared the Ravens were in position to get the ball back with a chance to win the game in the final minutes. But Roethlisberger connected with rookie receiver Antonio Brown for a remarkable sliding 58-yard catch in which Brown trapped the ball between his shoulder and helmet at the Baltimore 4. Mendenhall atoned for his earlier fumble with his second touchdown of the game to put Pittsburgh up 31–24 with 1:39 left. The Steelers could taste victory, but the Ravens would get one more shot.

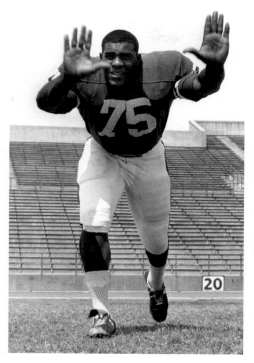

Pictured left was the first piece of the Steelers' great dynasty in the 1970s: Joe Greene. A consensus All-American at North Texas State University, Greene was the first selection in the 1969 NFL draft by brand-new Steelers coach Chuck Noll. He was chosen to his first of 10 Pro Bowls his rookie season. (Courtesy of the University of North Texas)

A first-round draft pick out of the University of Southern California in 2003, Troy Polamalu became one of the most exciting, athletic defensive players in the history of the team. Polamalu, the 2010 AFC Defensive Player of the Year, was an integral part of two Super Bowl championship teams. Pictured here at the parade to celebrate the 2008 Super Bowl XLIII title, he was at his best in the AFC championship that year when his interception touchdown return cemented the win for the Steelers. (Author's collection)

Art Rooney was a baseball player, champion boxer, and horseplayer extraordinaire. The most famous thing the "Chief" is known for, though, was purchasing a professional football team in 1933 for the city of Pittsburgh. The Pittsburgh Steelers became perhaps the city's most treasured possession. A statue honoring the team's founder is located outside Heinz Field. (Author's collection)

Forbes Field was the original home of the Pittsburgh Steelers. Built for the Pittsburgh Pirates in 1909, Forbes was the first steel-and-concrete facility in the National League. While it saw many championships for the Pirates and the local college football teams, Forbes only hosted one NFL playoff game, the 1947 eastern division championship, where Pittsburgh lost to the Eagles 21–0. (Courtesy of the Pittsburgh Pirates)

While known as one of the greatest defensive players in the history of the game, Hall of Famer Joe Greene was also known for something else in the 1980s: an actor in commercials. Seen here drinking a Coke on the sidelines while at North Texas State, Greene starred in what has become a legendary Coke commercial in 1980 during Super Bowl XIV. In 2012 he reprised the role in a Downy ad with comedienne Amy Sedaris. (Courtesy of the University of North Texas)

One of the most popular Steelers of all time is receiver Hines Ward. A third-round pick out of Georgia in 1998, Ward more than lived up to his potential, being the only Steeler ever to catch 1,000 passes in his career. He was at his best in 2005 when he was named the MVP in Super Bowl XL with five catches for 123 yards. He retired following the 2012 campaign. (Author's collection)

An aggressive linebacker out of Kent State, Jack Lambert came to the Pittsburgh Steelers in 1974. He turned out to be the final piece that transformed a very good defensive unit into a legendary one. No one was more intimidating than the 1974 NFL Defensive Rookie of the Year, the man they called "Count Dracula in Cleats." Lambert was elected to the Hall of Fame in 1990. (Courtesy of Kent State University)

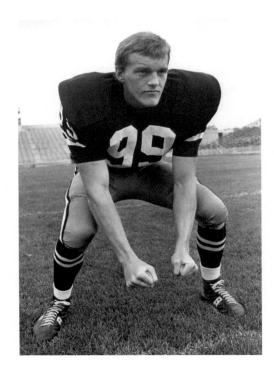

One of the greatest college football coaches of all time, John "Jock" Sutherland led the University of Pittsburgh to a 111–20–12 mark and five national championships. He was signed by Art Rooney to lead the Steelers in 1946 and within one year had them in a playoff for the eastern division championship. A year later he tragically died of brain cancer, and the club quickly returned to its losing ways. (Courtesy of the University of Pittsburgh)

Before the 1970 draft, the Chicago Bears and the Pittsburgh Steelers flipped a coin to see who would get the opportunity to draft a raw young quarterback from Louisiana Tech by the name of Terry Bradshaw. While he struggled for a few years, Bradshaw finally took hold of the starting job in 1974, helping to lead Pittsburgh to its first world championship. (Courtesy of Louisiana Tech University)

A starting quarterback from Northeast Louisiana University, Walter "Bubby" Brister showed flashes of greatness in Pittsburgh. Signing autographs for fans at training camp in Latrobe, Brister piloted the surprise Steelers team to a playoff run in 1989. He helped the club upset Houston in the first round that season and almost did the same against the Broncos in the next round. (Author's collection)

An All-American center at Duquesne University, center Mike Basrak didn't have far to move when he continued his pro career as the Steelers drafted him in the first round of the 1937 draft. Basrak, who was the MVP of the Orange Bowl for the Dukes in 1936, played two years for Pittsburgh, which was then known as the Pirates. (Courtesy of Duquesne University Athletics)

Seen here celebrating the Pittsburgh Steelers' sixth world championship in 2008, defensive coordinator Dick Lebeau had quite a hand in forming their two championship teams in the first decade of the twenty-first century. The man credited with creating the zone blitz, Lebeau is considered one of the finest defensive minds the league has ever seen. (Author's collection)

A first-round pick out of Ohio State in 2006, wide receiver Santonio Holmes was as well known for his occasional brushes with the law while in Pittsburgh as he was for his immense talent. He earned his spot in Steelers lore when he not only was named the MVP of Super Bowl XLIII but made arguably the most spectacular catch in league history, snagging the game-winning pass with 35 seconds left. (Author's collection)

In 1958 the Steelers began playing at Pitt Stadium, not far from their original home of Forbes Field. They played in both stadiums until 1964, when they moved into the facility full time. Pitt Stadium, which was built in 1925, hosted the franchise until 1969, the year before Three Rivers Stadium was built. While the Steelers had their worst season ever in 1969, the last win in Pitt Stadium was an exciting win against Detroit in Chuck Noll's first game. (Courtesy of the University of Pittsburgh)

By the late 1970s, quarterback Terry Bradshaw had become one of the best quarterbacks in the game. He was named MVP of Super Bowls XIII and XIV. Bradshaw passed for 932 yards in four Super Bowls while leading the Steelers to a record four championships. His impressive championship performances were one of the reasons he was elected to the Hall of Fame in 1989. (Courtesy of Louisiana Tech University)

In 1974, the Steelers chose Lynn Swann in the first round of the NFL draft. Three rounds later they took from Alabama A&M a less heralded receiver by the name of John Stallworth. By the time each of their careers ended, Swann's athleticism might have overshadowed Stallworth's less flamboyant steady style on the field, but despite that Stallworth became the all-time franchise leader in catches with 537. After years of waiting, Stallworth was inducted into the Hall of Fame in 2002. (Courtesy of Alabama A&M University)

Not many thought much when the Pittsburgh Steelers signed Willie Parker from North Carolina as an undrafted free agent in 2004. Within the next few years it looked like one of the shrewdest moves in franchise history, when he not only ran for 1,000 yards three times but set the single-game franchise record against the Browns with 223 yards in 2006. He also set the all-time Super Bowl record for longest run from scrimmage with a 75-yard touchdown jaunt in Super Bowl XL. (Author's collection)

After 37 years of toiling unsuccessfully in Forbes Field and Pitt Stadium, the Steelers moved into Three Rivers Stadium in 1970. For 31 years they delighted the Steeler Nation winning four AFC championships within its walls while the team went 182–72 playing there. In 2000 the team played its last game there, defeating the Washington Redskins 24–3. The facility was demolished on February 11, 2001. (Courtesy of the Pittsburgh Pirates)

For the better part of two decades the Pittsburgh Steelers had been searching for a replacement for Hall of Fame quarterback Terry Bradshaw. In 2004 the search came to an end when they drafted Ben Roethlisberger. Big Ben went 13–0 his rookie year and has led the Steelers to three Super Bowls since, winning two. In 2005 he became the youngest starting quarterback ever to win a Super Bowl. (Author's collection)

Pictured are the pride and joy of the Pittsburgh Steelers franchise, the Vince Lombardi Trophies that symbolize their Super Bowl championships. Shown here are the first five trophies they won. A sixth trophy was eventually added to the collection when they defeated the Arizona Cardinals 27–23 on February 1, 2009. The victory gave the franchise more Super Bowl victories than any other NFL team. (Author's collection)

A two-time All-American at Tennessee State, Jefferson Street Joe Gilliam nonetheless had to wait until the 11th round to be drafted by the Pittsburgh Steelers in 1972. While only the ninth quarterback taken in draft that year, by 1974 he was named the team's starting quarterback when they took on the Colts in the season opener. It made him only the second African American quarterback to begin the season starting for a team at QB. Within two years, drug addiction overtook him, and he was out of the league by 1976. (Courtesy of Tennessee State University)

After almost 70 years of sharing their home field with other teams, the Steelers finally had a place to call their own when they moved into Heinz Field in 2001. While the University of Pittsburgh does play football there, the Steelers are the main tenant and have rewarded fans with two AFC championships within its walls. Over 65,000 fans jam Heinz Field on Sundays during football season, as the Steelers have sold out every game they have ever played there, continuing the streak of home-game sellouts that began in 1972. (Author's collection)

Lifting the Vince Lombardi Trophy after their Super Bowl XLIII victory is linebacker James Harrison. Harrison was an undrafted rookie in 2002 who worked hard enough to eventually become a superstar with the team. Harrison was named the NFL Defensive Player of the Year in 2008 and set a Super Bowl record when he intercepted a Kurt Warner pass as the first half was coming to an end and returned it 100 yards, making it the longest play in Super Bowl history. (Author's collection)

Nicknamed Mean Joe Greene, Greene was at his best leading the Steelers to their first world championship in 1974. That year he changed his stance, lining up at a sharp angle between the guard and center to disrupt the blocking. Greene was dominant in the playoffs and Super Bowl, helping the Pittsburgh defense completely shut down their opponents. (Courtesy of the University of North Texas)

Monument honoring the "Immaculate Reception," which is located on the walkway between Heinz Field and PNC Park. It is located on the exact spot where Franco Harris remarkably snagged a deflected Terry Bradshaw and took it in for a touchdown to beat Oakland in the first round of the 1972 AFC Playoffs. NFL Films chose it as the greatest play of all time. The monument was dedicated on December 22, 2012, almost 40 years to the day that it occurred. (Author's collection)

A damaging unnecessary roughness penalty against Pittsburgh offensive lineman Chris Kemoeatu following the touchdown run pushed the Steelers back on the ensuing kickoff and helped set up Baltimore at the Pittsburgh 48 with just over a minute left. The Steelers' defense wasn't about to allow this one to slip away, collecting a sack and forcing three Flacco incompletions to secure a hard-earned playoff victory.

While there had been multiple heroes on both sides of the ball, Pittsburgh coach Mike Tomlin knew his quarterback had made the difference. "It's Ben," he said. "You give this guy an opportunity to snap it, he's capable of producing plays. It's not always how you draw it up, but he has a no-blink mentality. He is a competitor and a winner. And those guys follow him."[2]

And in following Roethlisberger like the Pied Piper, he'd once again led the Steelers to the brink of the Super Bowl.

BOXSCORE

TEAM	1st	2nd	3rd	4th	FINAL
Baltimore	14	7	0	3	24
Pittsburgh	7	0	14	10	31

TEAM	PLAY	SCORE
Pittsburgh	Mendenhall 1-yard run (Suisham kick)	0–7
Baltimore	Rice 14-yard run (Cundiff kick)	7–7
Baltimore	Redding 13-yard fumble return (Cundiff kick)	14–7
Baltimore	Heap 4-yard pass from Flacco (Cundiff kick)	21–7
Pittsburgh	Miller 9-yard pass from Roethlisberger (Suisham kick)	21–14
Pittsburgh	Ward 8-yard pass from Roethlisberger (Suisham kick)	21–21
Pittsburgh	Suisham 35-yard field goal	21–24
Baltimore	Cundiff 24-yard field goal	24–24
Pittsburgh	Mendenhall 2-yard run (Suisham kick)	24–31

RUSHING

PITT	ATT	YDS	AVE	TD
Mendenhall	20	46	2.3	2
Moore	2	12	6.0	0
Roethlisberger	6	11	1.8	0
Redman	1	4	4.0	0
Wallace	2	-2	-1.0	0

BALT	ATT	YDS	AVE	TD
Rice	12	32	2.8	1
McGahee	4	4	1.0	0
Flacco	2	-1	-1.0	0

RECEIVING

PITT	REC	YDS	AVE	TD
Miller	5	39	7.8	1
Sanders	4	54	13.5	0
Brown	3	75	25.0	0
Ward	3	25	8.3	1
Wallace	3	20	6.7	0
Mendenhall	1	13	13.0	0

BALT	REC	YDS	AVE	TD
Rice	7	32	4.6	0
Heap	3	43	14.3	1
Houshmandza-deh	3	38	12.7	0
McGahee	2	14	7.0	0
Boldin	1	-2	-2.0	0

PASSING

PITT	COMP	ATT	PCT	YDS	TD	INT
Roethlisberger	19	32	59.4	226	2	0

BALT	COMP	ATT	PCT	YDS	TD	INT
Flacco	16	30	53.3	125	1	1

STEELERS 30, BALTIMORE COLTS 0
SEPTEMBER 15, 1974

Jefferson Street Joe

Jefferson Street runs down the middle of the campus of Tennessee State University (TSU), the school's main thoroughfare. Through the university's century-long history, only one TSU alumnus has earned a nickname that celebrates that most famous road: Jefferson Street Joe Gilliam, who for a short time in 1974 set the National Football League on its ear after being named the starting quarterback for the Pittsburgh Steelers. His was an amazing story that unfortunately included a torturous fall.

In the early 1970s, African American quarterbacks were a rarity in professional football. Only two had ever started a professional football game: Marlin Briscoe for the Denver Broncos in 1968 and James Harris for the Buffalo Bills a year later. Five years later, an unlikely candidate joined them in gradually breaking down the wall of racial prejudice in sports.

Joe Gilliam was a record-setting quarterback at Tennessee State, but by the 11th round of the 1972 NFL Draft, he was still undrafted. Pittsburgh assistant director of player personnel Bill Nunn and head coach Chuck Noll had seen game films of Gilliam in college and decided that he was the best player available when the Steelers' turn came up.

The ninth quarterback taken in the draft, Gilliam soon became very well known. By 1974, with incumbent starter Terry Bradshaw struggling, Gilliam came to the forefront. He took advantage of a players' strike by crossing the picket line and leading Pittsburgh to an undefeated preseason record and earning the starting job for the opening game against the Baltimore Colts.

The national media descended on Pittsburgh to cover the historic event. *Sports Illustrated* ran it as a cover story under the headline "Pittsburgh's Black Quarterback." Journalistic icon Howard Cosell also covered the story, and Dan

Rather mentioned the development on the *CBS Evening News:* "There's . . . a sociological undertone with what the Steelers have been doing."[1]

Despite entering the season with Super Bowl hopes after two consecutive playoff seasons, the Steelers' prospects took a back seat to Gilliam's story.

As the game began, it became apparent that Gilliam was nervous. His first five passes fell incomplete, and he completed only two of his first 10. The sluggishness carried over to the rest of the team, and after the Steelers crept to a 3–0 lead, the Colts recovered a fumbled Pittsburgh punt return and were poised to surge ahead. But the famed Steel Curtain defense stepped up with a clutch goal-line stand that preserved the Pittsburgh lead. It was the beginning of the end for the Colts and gave Gilliam the spark he needed.

He led the offense on a 99-yard drive, the last 54 coming on a picture-perfect bomb to Lynn Swann for the first touchdown of what would become a remarkable career for the Hall of Fame receiver. Gerela missed the extra point, but the rout was on. Jefferson Street Joe closed out the half with another long scoring drive to make it 16–0.

His horrible beginning quickly turned into a remarkable afternoon. After his less-than-stellar start, Gilliam ended his day by hitting 15 of his last 21 passes and finished with 257 yards and two touchdown passes. Franco Harris and John Fuqua rounded out the scoring with touchdown runs in the second half, and Terry Hanratty, not Bradshaw, came in for fourth-quarter mop-up duty as Pittsburgh closed out a 30–0 win.

It was the beginning of what should have been a promising career, but after a fabulous game the next week against the Broncos where he threw for 348 yards, Jefferson Joe struggled. Though the Steelers were 4–1–1, Noll decided to replace Gilliam with Bradshaw and the rest was history.

Bradshaw went on to finally realize his potential, taking Pittsburgh to four Super Bowl victories in six seasons. Gilliam's career went in a different direction. Depressed over losing his job, he lapsed into a cocaine addiction that would plague him the rest of his life. He never started another NFL game and was cut by the Steelers after the 1975 season and was out of the league.

Gilliam was homeless for a couple years, selling his two Super Bowl rings for drug money. His father got his rings back and eventually his life began to turn around when he had an unfortunate relapse and died of a drug overdose on Christmas Day 2000, four days short of his 50th birthday.

Thus the opening game of the 1974 season has become about what could have been. Even Bradshaw later on admitted Gilliam may have had more potential than he did. "It easily could have been him instead of me," Bradshaw said. "He absolutely had what it took to lead the Steelers to the Super Bowl. He gave me my job back. I didn't earn it back. I didn't beat him out."[2] Ultimately, Gilliam's story became a tragedy, but its promising beginning inspired the African American quarterbacks who came after him—like Doug Williams who led the Tampa Bay Buccaneers to the playoffs five years after Gilliam's debut before becoming the first African American to win a Super Bowl as a starting quarterback. Even Kordell Stewart, the Steelers' starting quarterback when Gilliam died, remembered him as a pioneer—more like who he was on this September day in 1974 than the tragic figure he became.

BOXSCORE

TEAM	1st	2nd	3rd	4th	FINAL
Baltimore	0	0	0	0	0
Pittsburgh	3	13	7	7	30

TEAM	PLAY	SCORE
Pittsburgh	Gerela 31-yard field goal	0–3
Pittsburgh	Swann 54-yard pass from Gilliam (Gerela kick)	0–10
Pittsburgh	Lewis 4-yard pass from Gilliam (Gerela kick)	0–16
Pittsburgh	Harris 4-yard run (Gerela kick)	0–23
Pittsburgh	Fuqua 4-yard run (Gerela kick)	0–30

RUSHING

PITT	ATT	YDS	AVE	TD
Harris	13	49	3.8	1
Pearson	9	36	4.0	0
Fuqua	4	9	2.3	1
Davis	3	9	3.0	0

BALT	ATT	YDS	AVE	TD
Mitchell	9	44	4.9	0
McCauley	8	38	4.8	0
Olds	14	33	2.4	0
Jones	2	5	2.5	0
Andrews	1	-2	-2.0	0

RECEIVING

PITT	REC	YDS	AVE	TD
Grossman	3	52	17.3	0
Lewis	3	26	8.7	1
Harris	3	19	6.3	0
Swann	2	94	47.0	1
Davis	2	44	22.0	0
Stallworth	2	25	12.5	0
Fuqua	1	18	18.0	0
Brown	1	7	7.0	0
Pearson	1	4	4.0	0

BALT	REC	YDS	AVE	TD
Doughty	3	58	19.3	0
Chester	3	34	11.3	0
Mitchell	1	5	5.0	0
McCauley	1	3	3.0	0
Olds	1	2	2.0	0

PASSING

PITT	COMP	ATT	PCT	YDS	TD	INT
Gilliam	17	31	54.8	257	2	1
Hanratty	1	6	16.7	32	0	0

BALT	COMP	ATT	PCT	YDS	TD	INT
Jones	8	17	47.1	100	0	2
Domres	1	3	33.3	2	0	0

#18

STEELERS 16, OAKLAND RAIDERS 10
JANUARY 4, 1976

The Ice Man Cometh

In football, weather is the great equalizer. It can take a mismatch and turn it into a classic contest. But the elements have also impacted postseason games to the point that the conditions become the primary part of the story rather than the game itself.

In 1975, for example, the Oakland Raiders and the Pittsburgh Steelers fought through a tough regular season and met on a cold January day at Three Rivers Stadium for the championship of the American Football Conference, and yet the teams took a back seat to Mother Nature.

With the temperature in the mid-teens and a windchill factor below zero, 49,103 chilled members of Steeler Nation braved the conditions to see which team would advance to the Super Bowl and earn a trip to Miami—a particularly sweet prize on a day like this.

The frigid temperature was bad enough, but what happened after the grounds crew tried to account for it made things even more ridiculous. In an attempt to keep the field from becoming coated with ice, the tarp was placed over the Three Rivers turf a few days before the game and heaters were installed underneath.

The day before this game, the wind increased and the temperature dropped. The tarp began to rip at the edges, and over the course of the day, the field did indeed become icy, especially on the sidelines and in the end zones. The grounds crew then poured water on the turf in the hopes it would melt the ice. Instead, the water froze, making the field even more slippery.

When the teams arrived for the game, Raiders owner Al Davis was livid. After first being denied entrance into the stadium parking lot, he accused the Steelers of concocting the entire thing as a scheme to disable the potent

Oakland passing offense. He argued to NFL commissioner Pete Rozelle that the playing field was unplayable. But Rozelle allowed the game to go on. The Iceman had truly cometh to Pittsburgh.

With the ice came 60 minutes of the sloppiest football that the National Football League had ever seen, defined by 13 combined turnovers. Along the way, though, the Steelers and Raiders also produced a hard-fought, hard-hitting championship contest, complete with a frantic ending.

The Oakland defense rose to the occasion early, stopping the Steelers' offense twice on interceptions by Monte Johnson and Jack Tatum. But, led by injured Joe Greene, who'd missed the final five games of the regular season with a pinched nerve in his neck, the Pittsburgh defense was just a suffocating. "With Joe in there," said fellow defensive lineman Dwight White, "they didn't try to intimidate us. We took that away from them."[1]

The only scoring opportunity the Raiders had early on was a failed George Blanda field goal attempt from 38 yards out. The Steelers cashed in on a field-goal opportunity of their own, set up by a Mike Wagner interception, and took a 3–0 lead in the second quarter.

As the game wore on, it became as bitter as the temperature, reflected by a vicious hit by Oakland's George Atkinson on Lynn Swann that sent the Steelers' receiver to the hospital. Trying to get even was Pittsburgh linebacker Jack Lambert, who not only recovered three fumbles but got his uniform caked with his opponents' blood.

The 3–0 score held up until the fourth quarter, when both offenses finally took off. On the second play of the final quarter, Lambert recovered a Clarence Davis fumble to give the Steelers possession at the Oakland 25. Receiver John Stallworth then threw a key block on Tatum that provided enough daylight for Franco Harris to race down the icy sideline for a touchdown and a 10–0 lead.

Oakland quarterback Kenny Stabler then led the Raiders on a 60-yard touchdown drive to cut the lead to three, but Pittsburgh's L. C. Greenwood halted the Raiders' newfound momentum, causing a fumble that Lambert recovered. Moments later Terry Bradshaw threw a 20-yard scoring pass to Stallworth, who broke free when both Oakland defenders covering him slipped and fell. Pittsburgh muffed the snap on the extra point, but they still led 16–7.

The frigid fans began planning a return trip to the Super Bowl, but a few tense moments still remained. With less than two minutes to play and the Steelers trying to run out the clock, Oakland's Ted Hendricks recovered a fumble by Harris to give the Raiders new life. Oakland drove to the Pittsburgh 24, where on third down coach John Madden sent in Blanda with 17 seconds left to kick a field goal and cut the lead to six. The Raiders had extended the game but now had to recover the ensuing onside kick and then pull off a miracle play to pull out a victory.

Oakland did in fact recover the onside kick, and quarterback Ken Stabler then launched a 35-yard pass to speedy wideout Cliff Branch, who caught it at the 15 but was gang tackled by Mel Blount and the Pittsburgh defense as time expired. The jubilant Steelers returned to their warm locker room after securing their second straight AFC championship.

While Stallworth, Harris, Lambert, and Wagner were all Steelers heroes in this game, perhaps the most deciding aspect of the game was the cold and the ice and the slippery conditions that resulted. As Al Davis had feared, the elements had rendered his high-powered offense useless and sent the Raiders back home to sunny California from Pittsburgh without a title for the second time in three years.

BOXSCORE

TEAM	1st	2nd	3rd	4th	FINAL
Oakland	0	0	0	10	10
Pittsburgh	0	3	0	13	16

TEAM	PLAY	SCORE
Pittsburgh	Gerela 36-yard field goal	0–3
Pittsburgh	Harris 25-yard run (Serela kick)	0–10
Oakland	Siani 14-yard pass from Stabler (Blanda kick)	7–10
Pittsburgh	Stallworth 20-yard pass from Bradshaw (kick failed)	7–16
Oakland	Blanda 41-yard field goal	10–16

RUSHING

PITT	ATT	YDS	AVE	TD
Harris	27	79	2.9	1
Bradshaw	2	22	11.0	0
Bleier	10	16	1.6	0

RUSHING

OAK	ATT	YDS	AVE	TD
Banaszak	8	33	4.1	0
Hubbard	10	30	3.0	0
Davis	13	29	2.2	0
Phillips	1	1	1.0	0

RECEIVING

PITT	REC	YDS	AVE	TD
Harris	5	58	11.6	0
Grossman	4	36	9.0	0
Swann	2	45	22.5	0
Stallworth	2	30	15.0	1
Lewis	1	33	33.0	0
Brown	1	13	13.0	0

OAK	REC	YDS	AVE	TD
Siani	5	80	16.0	1
Casper	5	67	13.4	0
Branch	2	56	28.0	0
Banaszak	2	12	6.0	0
Moore	2	12	6.0	0
Hart	1	16	16.0	0
Davis	1	3	3.0	0

PASSING

PITT	COMP	ATT	PCT	YDS	TD	INT
Bradshaw	15	25	60.0	215	1	3

OAK	COMP	ATT	PCT	YDS	TD	INT
Stabler	18	42	42.9	246	1	2

STEELERS 34, OAKLAND RAIDERS 28
SEPTEMBER 17, 1972

The Year of the Steelers

For 39 years the Pittsburgh Steelers had been mired in mediocrity. In their good years, they hovered around the break-even mark. In the rest, they labored at the bottom of the National Football League standings, hoping that one day they would figure out a way to climb out of their seemingly never-ending hole. After Chuck Noll was hired as head coach in 1969, things gradually began to turn around, and then on opening day 1972, the Steelers finally emerged as a title contender, beginning what Pittsburgh columnist Phil Musick conjectured would be the year of the Steelers.

Pittsburgh set the tone in the preseason, going 4–1–1 while giving up only 63 points. The offense was given an infusion of power with their top draft pick, Franco Harris, a powerful running back out of Penn State. By year's end, Harris would make the Steelers' offense extremely effective, but if they were to make the next step it would be on the heels of their developing defense.

The Steelers would receive a real test in the opener, facing a perennially powerful Oakland team that had uncharacteristically missed the playoffs in 1971 and was hungry for a return trip.

But from the outset, the Pittsburgh defense dominated, making Oakland quarterback Kenny Stabler's first NFL start a miserable experience. Linebacker Chuck Beatty picked off Stabler deep in Oakland territory early in the first, though the Steelers returned the favor with a Terry Bradshaw interception moments later. But the Pittsburgh special teams would make up for the miscue when Henry Davis blocked a punt and returned it five yards for a touchdown and a 7–0 Pittsburgh lead.

The Steelers' defense continued to haunt Stabler when linebacker Jack Ham intercepted another pass, setting up a Terry Bradshaw scoring scamper from

20 yards out to increase the advantage to two touchdowns. Beatty then picked off his second pass of the half to set up a Steelers field goal that made it 17–0.

Oakland coach John Madden had seen enough, replacing young Stabler with 45-year-old George Blanda, who stopped the bleeding temporarily. A Raiders interception late in the second quarter gave them possession near midfield, and Blanda quickly marched his team into the end zone to cut the margin to 10 points at the intermission.

The Steelers quickly regained the momentum early in the third quarter when Oakland punter Jerry DePoyster muffed the snap on a punt, and the Steelers took over at the Raiders 7. Roy Gerela booted another field goal to make it 20–7, and then Bradshaw spearheaded another scoring drive, capping it with his second touchdown run of the afternoon to put the home team up by 20 points as the third quarter came to a close.

In desperation, Madden yanked Blanda and replaced him with Daryl "The Mad Bomber" Lamonica, who quickly cut the lead to 27–14 with a 24-yard touchdown pass to Mike Siani. Just as suddenly, Bradshaw restored the 20-point lead with a 57-yard bomb to Ron Shanklin. But Lamonica wasn't done. And neither were the Raiders.

A pass interference call on Pittsburgh defensive back Lee Calland at the Oakland 1 set up a touchdown run by Don Highsmith, and then Lamonica hit Siani for a 70-yard scoring bomb with 38 seconds left to pull Oakland within six points. The Steelers recovered the ensuing onside kick, but still the game wasn't wrapped up. They faced fourth and one in Oakland territory with 30 seconds left, and Noll opted to go for it rather than risk a blocked punt. The Raiders jumped offside before the snap, giving the Steelers the first down and enabling them to melt the final seconds and clinch an impressive opening-day victory.

The win prompted Musick to ask the question if it was finally the Steelers' year. Three months later after they captured the AFC central division championship with an 11–3 mark, winning their first title of any kind in their 40-year history, that answer was given a resounding yes; 1972 was truly the year of the Steelers.

BOXSCORE

TEAM	1st	2nd	3rd	4th	FINAL
Oakland	0	7	0	21	28
Pittsburgh	14	3	10	7	34

TEAM	PLAY	SCORE
Pittsburgh	Davis 5-yard blocked kick (Gerela kick)	0–7
Pittsburgh	Bradshaw 20-yard run (Gerela kick)	0–14
Pittsburgh	Gerela 48-yard field goal	0–17
Oakland	Chester 26-yard pass from Blanda (Blanda kick)	7–17
Pittsburgh	Gerela 8-yard field goal	7–20
Pittsburgh	Bradshaw 2-yard run (Gerela kick)	7–27
Oakland	Siani 24-yard pass from Lamonica (Blanda kick)	14–27
Pittsburgh	Shanklin 57-yard pass from Bradshaw (Gerela kick)	14–34
Oakland	Highsmith 1-yard run (Blanda kick)	21–34
Oakland	Siani 70-yard pass from Lamonica (Blanda kick)	28–34

RUSHING

PITT	ATT	YDS	AVE	TD
Pearson	18	54	3.0	0
Bradshaw	7	49	7.0	2
Harris	10	28	2.8	0
Davis	4	5	1.3	0
Fuqua	2	5	2.5	0

OAK	ATT	YDS	AVE	TD
Hubbard	15	58	3.9	0
Smith	6	26	4.3	0
Lamonica	2	15	7.5	0
Queen	1	6	6.0	0
Stabler	1	0	0.0	0
Highsmith	5	-8	-1.6	1

RECEIVING

PITT	REC	YDS	AVE	TD
McMakin	3	39	13.0	0
Harris	2	16	8.0	0
Shanklin	1	57	57.0	0
Pearson	1	12	12.0	0

OAK	REC	YDS	AVE	TD
Siani	4	111	27.8	2
Moore	4	41	10.3	0
Chester	3	63	21.0	1
Biletnikoff	3	39	13.0	0
Highsmith	1	22	22.0	0
Smith	1	18	18.0	0
Hubbard	1	-4	-4.0	0

PASSING

PITT	COMP	ATT	PCT	YDS	TD	INT
Bradshaw	7	17	41.2	124	1	3

OAK	COMP	ATT	PCT	YDS	TD	INT
Stabler	5	12	40.0	54	0	3
Blanda	4	11	36.4	64	1	0
Lamonica	8	10	80.0	172	2	0

STEELERS 24, NEW YORK JETS 19
JANUARY 23, 2011

A Guarantee Gone Bad

The New York Jets were a confident bunch coming into the 2010 AFC Championship at Heinz Field. Not only had they beaten the Steelers on this very same turf a month before, but they just had defeated two of the best quarterbacks in NFL history to advance through the playoffs.

With victories over Peyton Manning and the Indianapolis Colts 17–16 in the first round and then over the Tom Brady–led New England Patriots the following week, the Jets were now one win away from returning to the Super Bowl for the first time in 42 years, when quarterback Joe Namath delivered a stunning upset of the heavily favored Baltimore Colts in Super Bowl III.

After what they'd accomplished the previous two weeks, the Jets were certain they would emerge victorious. Receiver Braylon Edwards brashly declared that the Steelers' Ben Roethlisberger would be the next star quarterback they'd take down. Fellow Jets wideout Santonio Holmes, who'd won a Super Bowl with the Steelers two years earlier, was looking for revenge against his former team. "I got a chance to beat those guys the first time around," Holmes said. "I don't care about the Steelers right now. . . . If we win the Super Bowl, that's a slap back in [their] face for trading me."[1] New York head coach Rex Ryan, who usually is a much more boastful sort, had a tad less braggadocio but was confident nonetheless. "If they want to put them [the Steeler six Super Bowl trophies] on the field," he said, "we'll play them, too. We want the t-shirt. We want the hat. We want the trophy."[2]

Brash confidence and guarantees always make the week between championship clashes more interesting and often fire up the fans, but come game time, you still have to play the contest. In this instance, the experience and talent of the Pittsburgh Steelers, coupled with home-field advantage, trumped any psychological advantage the cocky Jets thought they had.

The Steelers took control early and quickly showing the Jets they were in for a long evening. On the first drive of the game, Pittsburgh drove 15 plays in nine minutes, with running back Rashard Mendenhall pounding through the right side of the Pittsburgh offensive line eight times on the way to a one-yard touchdown run.

Meanwhile, the New York offense was stymied by the Steelers' hungry defense, and Pittsburgh added to its lead with a field goal early in the second quarter. On their next possession, the Steelers once again put together a long, bruising drive downfield. Roethlisberger completed key passes to Heath Miller, Emmanuel Sanders, and Mendenhall before taking it in himself from the New York 2 to make it 17–0. The rout, it appeared, was on.

While the Pittsburgh offense appeared unstoppable, it suffered a serious blow when rookie center Maurkice Pouncey went down with a sprained ankle. It didn't seem it would matter when the Steelers' defense appeared to put the nail in the New York coffin two plays after Roethlisberger's touchdown. Ike Taylor sacked Jets quarterback Mark Sanchez and forced a fumble. William Gay picked it up and ran 19 yards into the end zone to make it 24–0 with a little over a minute left in the half.

For all intents and purposes, it appeared the game was over, and the last 31 minutes would be just a formality witnessed by a record crowd of 66,662. But no one told the Jets. With the Steelers dropping into a prevent defense, Sanchez took the Jets down the field to set up a field goal in the last minute of the half to make it 24–3 at the intermission. The Jets picked up where they left off to start the third quarter, quickly moving downfield and cutting the margin to two touchdowns on a long scoring bomb to Holmes. The Jets' confidence was returning, while the Steelers appeared dazed. The defense was on its heels, and the Pittsburgh offense was no longer moving the chains as the last quarter began. When the Jets drove to the Pittsburgh 2 with 8:39 left, it appeared a game that started out as a blowout might go down to the wire.

With their backs against the wall, the Pittsburgh defense, pushed around for the last two quarters, stood tall with a goal-line stand that halted the Jets' momentum. However, the offense gave it right back when Roethlisberger fumbled the ball in the end zone moments later. He landed on it before the Jets could, giving New York a safety rather than a touchdown, but the Jets were now two points closer and would get the ball back. They quickly drove back downfield, and a short Sanchez touchdown pass cut the Pittsburgh lead to 24–19 with three minutes to play. The Steelers' next possession became the most important one of the day.

With all three of their time-outs remaining, the Jets decided to forgo the onside kick in the hope that their defense would get them the ball back for a chance to win the game. Roethlisberger was able to get a quick first down on a 14-yard completion to Miller, but with two minutes left, and the ball on the New York 40, the Steelers faced a third and six. Conventional thinking dictated that Pittsburgh should run the ball, melt the clock, and then punt to pin the Jets deep in their territory. Instead of playing it safe, Steelers head coach Mike Tomlin decided to go for the first down and clinch victory then and there. Instead of simply handing off to Mendenhall, who'd gained only 26 yards in the second half after piling up 95 in the first, Roethlisberger tossed a pass to rookie Antonio Brown, who grabbed it for a 14-yard gain and the AFC championship-clinching first down. Roethlisberger kneeled out the final seconds, and the Steelers were headed back to the Super Bowl for a record eighth time.

The Jets' guarantees had gone for naught. Afterward, Rex Ryan didn't regret his players' brashness the week before, and he himself made bold predictions for 2011. "We don't need to apologize to anybody," he said. "We'll be back, you'll see."[3]

Conversely, the Steelers had treated the entire episode like professionals, like a championship team that had been here before. They'd made no guarantees, no bold predictions. They'd simply shown up.

And won.

BOXSCORE

TEAM	1st	2nd	3rd	4th	FINAL
New York	0	3	7	9	19
Pittsburgh	7	17	0	0	24

TEAM	PLAY	SCORE
Pittsburgh	Mendenhall 1-yard run (Suisham kick)	0–7
Pittsburgh	Suisham 20-yard field goal	0–10
Pittsburgh	Roethlisberger 2-yard run (Suisham kick)	0–17
Pittsburgh	Gay 19-yard fumble return (Suisham kick)	0–24
New York	Folk 42-yard field goal	3–24
New York	Holmes 45-yard pass from Sanchez (Folk kick)	10–24
New York	Safety Devito tackled Roethlisberger in end zone	12–24
New York	Cotchery 4-yard pass from Sanchez	19–24

RUSHING

PITT	ATT	YDS	AVE	TD
Mendenhall	27	121	4.5	1
Redman	4	27	6.8	0
Roethlisberger	11	21	1.9	1
Moore	1	-3	-3.0	0

NY	ATT	YDS	AVE	TD
Greene	9	52	5.8	0
Tomlinson	9	16	1.8	0
Sanchez	3	6	2.0	0
Cotchery	1	-4	-4.0	0

RECEIVING

PITT	REC	YDS	AVE	TD
Miller	2	38	19.0	0
Mendenhall	2	32	16.0	0
Ward	2	14	7.0	0
Sanders	1	20	20.0	0
Brown	1	14	14.0	0
Moore	1	9	9.0	0
Wallace	1	6	6.0	0

RECEIVING

NY	REC	YDS	AVE	TD
Keller	8	64	8.0	0
Cotchery	5	33	6.6	1
Edwards	3	50	16.7	0
Holmes	2	61	30.5	1
Smith	2	25	12.5	0

PASSING

PIT	COMP	ATT	PCT	YDS	TD	INT
Roethlisberger	10	19	52.6	133	0	2

NY	COMP	ATT	PCT	YDS	TD	INT
Sanchez	20	33	60.6	233	2	0

STEELERS 27, HOUSTON OILERS 13
JANUARY 6, 1980

A Case for Instant Replay

In the minds of the 1979 Houston Oilers and their witty head coach Bum Phillips, their AFC Championship clash against the Pittsburgh Steelers happened seven years too soon. Had the game occurred following the 1985 campaign, on a controversial play, game officials would have been able to access the instant-replay video system that would later become an accepted—almost embraced—part of the game.

Unfortunately for the Oilers, in January 1980, no such system existed, and it cost them. With the Oilers down 17–10, quarterback Dan Pastorini seemed to have tied the game with a touchdown pass to Mike Renfro, who'd apparently taken the ball away from Pittsburgh defensive back Ron Johnson before going out of bounds. Side judge Donald Orr disagreed, claiming Renfro did not have possession before he went out of bounds. The referees gathered and discussed Orr's call, but with no instant replay to tell definitively whether or not Orr's call was correct, the call stood. Instead of the turning point of the game, the Oilers saw their Super Bowl dreams begin to fade.

They'd entered this championship contest with high expectations. After being obliterated by the Steelers in the conference title a year earlier, the Oilers brought new confidence into the 1979 rematch.

While close, the Steelers were not quite at the same level as they were in 1978. Offensively, they were actually more explosive, leading the NFL in scoring with 416 points and yards gained with 6,258. On the defensive side, age and injuries were starting to wreak havoc with what was once one of the greatest units in league history. While they still finished fifth in the NFL in points given up, it was 67 more than they'd allowed the prior year. They'd also yielded more than 30 on four occasions after not allowing 30 points in a game at all in '78.

To make matters worse, they'd lost to the Oilers in the second-to-last game of the season, further changing the dominant attitude of the team and fueling Houston's confidence.

Reflecting these changes, the Oilers came out much more effectively in the 1979 matchup. Early in the game, Pittsburgh quarterback Terry Bradshaw tossed an errant pass that ended up in the hands of Oilers defensive back Vernon Perry, who returned the ball 75 yards for a touchdown to give Houston the early 7–0 lead.

After the teams exchanged field goals, the Steelers surged ahead on a pair of Bradshaw touchdown passes—one to tight end Bennie Cunningham and one to John Stallworth—to make it 17–10. The lead persevered until Renfro's controversial non-touchdown catch in the third quarter, and Houston had to settle for a 23-yard Fritch three-pointer to bring the Oilers within 17–13.

Though Houston had pulled within striking distance, the Oilers' attitude was damaged by the missed opportunity. It was a moment of adversity, when champions pick their heads up and push forward. Houston sulked while Pittsburgh took it to the next level.

With the Oilers distracted, the Steelers marched 55 yards to set up a 39-yard Matt Bahr field goal to restore their touchdown lead. On their ensuing possession, the Oilers picked up a couple of first downs before Guido Merkens fumbled and Pittsburgh's Donnie Shell recovered. Moments later, Rocky Bleier burst into the end zone from four yards for the game-clinching touchdown.

When it was over, Pittsburgh celebrated its fourth AFC championship in six seasons while Houston went home empty once again, longing for the creation of instant replay.

BOXSCORE

TEAM	1st	2nd	3rd	4th	FINAL
Houston	7	3	0	3	13
Pittsburgh	3	14	0	10	27

TEAM	PLAY	SCORE
Houston	Perry 75-yard interception return (Fritsch kick)	7–0
Pittsburgh	Bahr 21-yard field goal	7–3
Houston	Fritsch 21-yard field goal	10–3
Pittsburgh	Cunningham 16 yard pass from Bradshaw (Bahr kick)	10–10
Pittsburgh	Stallworth 20-yard pass from Bradshaw (Bahr kick)	10–17
Houston	Fritsch 23-yard field goal	13–17
Pittsburgh	Bahr 39-yard field goal	13–20
Pittsburgh	Bleier 4-yard run (Bahr kick)	13–27

RUSHING

PITT	ATT	YDS	AVE	TD
Harris	21	85	4.0	0
Bleier	13	52	4.0	1
Bradshaw	1	25	25.0	0
Thornton	1	-1	-1.0	0

HOU	ATT	YDS	AVE	TD
Campbell	17	15	0.9	0
Wilson	4	9	2.3	0
Caster	1	0	0.0	0

RECEIVING

PITT	REC	YDS	AVE	TD
Harris	6	50	8.3	0
Swann	4	64	16.0	0
Stallworth	3	52	17.3	1
Bleier	3	39	13.0	0
Cunningham	2	14	7.0	1

RECEIVING

HOU	REC	YDS	AVE	TD
Wilson	7	60	8.6	0
Carpenter	5	23	4.6	0
Renfro	3	52	17.3	0
Coleman	2	46	23.0	0
Merkens	1	12	12.0	0
Campbell	1	11	11.0	0
Barber	1	8	8.0	0

PASSING

PITT	COMP	ATT	PCT	YDS	TD	INT
Bradshaw	18	30	60.0	219	2	1

HOU	COMP	ATT	PCT	YDS	TD	INT
Pastorini	19	28	67.9	203	0	1
Nielsen	1	1	100.0	9	0	0

STEELERS 24, DENVER BRONCOS 17
DECEMBER 30, 1984

A Monumental Upset

Through each year of the 1980s, members of one of the greatest dynasties in the history of the National Football League were leaving the team, one by one. Super Bowl memories were being replaced by Hall of Fame speeches as the dynasty was sputtering on fumes.

Even with the downward trend, 1984 proved to be a memorable season for the Steelers. While their 9–7 record was not spectacular, they notched impressive road victories over the Los Angeles Raiders and San Francisco to pave the road to the playoffs.

Their prize was a trip to Mile High Stadium to face the second-seeded Denver Broncos. Finishing 13–3 in the tough AFC West, the Broncos would provide the Steelers with a most difficult task at one of the most difficult places to play in the NFL.

Led by second-year quarterback John Elway, who was beginning to display the talent that would make him one of the greatest QB's ever to stand behind center, and a respectable defense, Denver was a very well-rounded team that had won its final 10 games to soar into the playoffs with momentum and was a clear favorite in the contest. The Steelers, meanwhile, were led offensively by Mark Malone, who'd finally staked his claim to the starting quarterback job, and a handful of leftovers from the Steel Curtain days. While the makeup of the teams was comparable, the Broncos were the clear favorite.

Pittsburgh did little to help its own cause with two first-quarter fumbles. Denver missed a field goal after the first but cashed in the second for a John Elway touchdown pass to make it 7–0. It was at that point the Steelers picked themselves up and showed Denver that, if nothing else, this game would not be a rout. With the Broncos driving deep into Pittsburgh territory and poised to go up by two touchdowns, Pittsburgh nose tackle Gerry Dunn picked off an errant Elway toss to swing the momentum. The rejuvenated Steelers took the ball back downfield to set up a 28-yard Gary Anderson field goal.

Their confidence restored and momentum now squarely on their side, the Steelers went on a 78-yard drive that was dominated by running back Frank Pollard, who ran three times for 44 yards on the drive before finishing it with a one-yard touchdown plunge to make it 10–7, Pittsburgh, with just over a minute left in the half.

Pittsburgh then started the second half the same way they started the first—with a critical mistake. They allowed a blocked punt following the first possession of the third quarter, and the Broncos took over at the Pittsburgh 4. The Steelers' defense held, and the Broncos settled for a game-tying field goal. Minutes later, however, Denver sent the Mile High crowd into hysterics with a 20-yard touchdown pass from Elway to Steve Watson to make it 17–10.

Just when it appeared the Steelers would fold up the tents, they clawed back into the game. Malone, playing on a sprained ankle, marched his offense 66 yards with a handful of completions to rookie wideout Louis Lipps. His last catch was a 10-yarder in which he carried Denver defensive back Louis Wright into the end zone for the tying touchdown as the third quarter wound down.

The score remained tied well into the fourth, with the Pittsburgh defense hanging tough and frustrating Elway. The offense, meanwhile, continued to have success moving the ball, though it was for naught when Anderson missed a field goal—his second miss of the day—that would have given Pittsburgh the lead.

The game looked like it was headed to overtime until Elway made another mistake, one that put the Steelers in a position to pull off the upset. Eric Williams picked off a pass and returned it to the Denver 5. Pollard smashed into the end zone from two yards out to make it 24–17 with 1:59 remaining.

In the years to come, Elway would build a reputation for leading clutch drives in this situation, but in 1984, he was still a young, relatively inexperienced quarterback and was unable to move the ball on the Pittsburgh defense. The Steelers hung on for this incredible playoff victory, which proved to be the last postseason win of the Steel Curtain era.

Head Coach Chuck Noll, who built the dynasty, was impressed as it made its last great stand. "No doubt the mistakes they made early could have destroyed a football team," Noll said. "Our comeback shows what this team is made of." It was made up of heart and character, giving the Steeler Nation one last great moment with this monumental upset.[1]

BOXSCORE

TEAM	1st	2nd	3rd	4th	FINAL
Pittsburgh	0	10	7	7	24
Denver	7	0	10	0	17

TEAM	PLAY	SCORE
Denver	Wright 9-yard pass from Elway (Karlis kick)	0–7
Pittsburgh	Anderson 28-yard field goal	3–7
Pittsburgh	Pollard 1-yard run (Anderson kick)	10–7
Denver	Karlis 21-yard field goal	10–10
Denver	Watson 20-yard pass from Elway (Karlis kick)	10–17
Pittsburgh	Lipps 10-yard pass from Malone (Anderson kick)	17–17
Pittsburgh	Pollard 2-yard run (Anderson kick)	24–17

RUSHING

PITT	ATT	YDS	AVE	TD
Pollard	16	99	6.2	2
Abercrombie	17	75	4.4	0
Veals	1	1	1.0	0
Lipps	1	0	0.0	0
Malone	5	-6	-1.2	0

DEN	ATT	YDS	AVE	TD
Winder	15	37	2.5	0
Elway	4	16	4.0	0
Willhite	1	1	1.0	0
Parros	1	0	0.0	0
Watson	1	-3	-3.0	0

RECEIVING

PITT	REC	YDS	AVE	TD
Lipps	5	86	17.2	1
Pollard	4	48	12.0	0
Stallworth	3	38	12.7	0
Abercrombie	3	18	6.0	0
Cunningham	1	19	19.0'	0
Thompson	1	15	15.0	0

DEN	REC	YDS	AVE	TD
Watson	11	177	16.1	1
Winder	4	22	5.5	0
Wright	2	16	8.0	0
Willhite	2	12	6.0	0
Alexander	1	9	9.0	0

PASSING

PITT	COMP	ATT	PCT	YDS	TD	INT
Malone	17	28	60.7	224	1	0

DEN	COMP	ATT	PCT	YDS	TD	INT
Elway	19	37	51.3	184	2	2
Willhite	1	1	100.0	52	0	0

STEELERS 63, NEW YORK GIANTS 7
NOVEMBER 30, 1952

The Offensive Explosion

In their long history, the Pittsburgh Steelers have had many Hall of Fame players on offense: Terry Bradshaw, Franco Harris, Lynn Swann, Ben Roethlisberger, and Hines Ward just to name a few. But it was the unlikely trio of Lynn Chadnois, Jim Finks, and Dick Hensley that combined for the single greatest scoring day in Steelers history on a November Sunday in 1952.

Up to that point it hadn't been the best of seasons for the Steelers. They lost their first four games and six of the first eight. But the Steelers were better than their 2–6 record, reflected by five of their defeats coming by a combined 12 points.

Pittsburgh was led by fourth-year quarterback Jim Finks, who was in his first year as a starter and was improving as the year went on. With Finks finding his footing, Pittsburgh went into a Week Ten encounter with momentum against the first-place New York Giants following a 17–14 win over the Chicago Cardinals, which gave them their third victory. New York, one of the traditional powers in the league, was 6–3, led by one of the best defenses in the league that had allowed only 107 points in the first nine contests for an average of less than 12 points per game. No one could have foreseen the ambush that was about to take place at Forbes Field.

Many in the sparse crowd of 15,140 hadn't evened found their seats when Chadnois took the opening kickoff 91 yards for a touchdown and a 7–0 Pittsburgh lead. Seven minutes later Chadnois upped the score to 14–0 when he scored on a five-yard touchdown run, capping a nice drive on which the Pittsburgh offensive line began to destroy the vaunted New York front wall.

After gaining a two-touchdown advantage, Pittsburgh head coach Joe Bach opened up the playbook, and Finks started making big plays. First he hit Elbie

Nickel—the receiver who by game's end would set the franchise record for yards receiving in a season—for a 21-yard score to make it 21–0. Finks then connected with Ray Mathews on a 42-yard bomb to turn the game into a rout at the half.

Early in the third quarter, Pittsburgh raised the lead to five touchdowns when Finks tossed his third scoring pass in a little over a quarter. This one went to Dick Hensley from 25 yards, making it 35–0. For as many impressive performances as there were on this day, probably the most amazing belonged to Hensley. The former Giant, who would only have 19 catches in his entire professional football career, caught seven of them in this game for 154 yards and the only two touchdowns of his NFL career.

After Henley stretched the lead to five touchdowns, the Giants scored their only points of the afternoon. The Pittsburgh defense, which had been as dominant as its offense, had knocked out both New York quarterbacks, forcing coach Steve Owen to use defensive back Tom Landry behind center. The future Hall of Fame coach for the Dallas Cowboys was a miserable five-for 24 passing but delivered the Giants' only touchdown on a pass to Bill Stribling, who made a brilliant catch, and then as he was about to be tackled, pitched it to Joe Scott. Scott in turn tossed it back to Stribling, who ran it the remaining 35 yards for the touchdown. It would be the lone high point for the Giants of the day.

On the first play of the final quarter, Finks found Henley with a long 60-yard pass for the team's sixth touchdown. Then soon after that, Dale Dodrill blocked a punt, and George Hays took it the final three yards to make it an incredible 49–7. Bach took out Finks after his 12-completion, 254-yard, 4-touchdown performance and replaced him with kicker and backup quarterback Gary Kerkorian. Kerkorian picked up where Finks left off, finding future Hall of Famer Jack Butler for a 20-yard touchdown pass to extend the lead to 56–7. Ed Modzelewski put his name in the Steelers' record book as he rammed the ball in from the 3 to push Pittsburgh over the 60-point plateau.

It was an unexpectedly brilliant performance that saw nine franchise records broken, including points scored (63), passes intercepted (7), passing yards in a game (315), and touchdown passes in a game (5). It was a day in which a group of players who otherwise would have been forgotten etched their name into team history.

BOXSCORE

TEAM	1st	2nd	3rd	4th	FINAL
New York	0	0	7	0	7
Pittsburgh	14	14	7	28	63

TEAM	PLAY	SCORE
Pittsburgh	Chadnois 91-yard run (Kerkorian kick)	0–7
Pittsburgh	Chadnois 5-yard run (Kerkorian kick)	0–14
Pittsburgh	Nickel 21-yard pass from Finks (Kerkorian kick)	0–21
Pittsburgh	Mathews 42-yard pass from Finks (Kerkorian kick)	0–28
Pittsburgh	Hensley 25-yard pass from Finks (Kerkorian kick)	0–35
New York	Stribling 55-yard pass from Landry (Poole kick)	7–35
Pittsburgh	Hensley 60-yard pass from Finks (Kerkorian kick)	7–42
Pittsburgh	Hays 3-yard blocked punt return (Mathews kick)	7–49
Pittsburgh	Butler 20-yard pass from Kerkorian (Kerkorian kick)	7–56
Pittsburgh	Modzelewski 3-yard run (Kerkorian kick)	7–63

RUSHING

PITT	ATT	YDS	AVE	TD
Modzelewski	6	35	5.8	1
Chadnois	11	30	2.7	1
Kerkorian	1	20	20.0	0
Calvin	4	19	4.8	0
Rogel	5	16	3.2	0
Spinks	1	3	3.0	0
Shipkey	1	1	1.0	0
Finks	1	1	1.0	0
Mathews	5	-2	-0.4	0

RUSHING

NY	ATT	YDS	AVE	TD
Landry	4	20	5.0	0
Price	9	3	0.3	0
Amberg	1	2	2.0	0
Scott	5	0	0.0	0
Conerly	1	-10	-10.0	0

PASSING

PITT	COMP	ATT	PCT	YDS	TD	INT
Finks	12	24	50.0	254	4	N/A
Kerkorian	2	4	50.0	47	1	N/A
Brady	1	2	50.0	14	0	N/A
Mathews	0	1	00.0	0	0	N/A

NY	COMP	ATT	PCT	YDS	TD	INT
Landry	4	25	16.0	106	1	N/A
Conerly	4	7	57.1	37	0	N/A
Benners	3	7	42.9	32	0	N/A

STEELERS 21, INDIANAPOLIS COLTS 18
JANUARY 15, 2006

Our Idiot Kicker

Except for a hiccup in 2001 when they finished 6–10, the Indianapolis Colts had been the one of the most dominant teams in the National Football League in the first decade of the twenty-first century. Led by quarterback Peyton Manning and quiet, classy head coach Tony Dungy, the Colts had also been a franchise essentially void of controversy, aside from a minor one following the 2002 campaign that received quite a bit of media attention.

In an interview with a Canadian television station, Colts kicker Mike Vanderjagt ripped Manning and Dungy, claiming they should both show more emotion on and off the field. The comments infuriated Manning, even after the kicker apologized. In an interview at the Pro Bowl, Manning addressed the issue, claiming Vanderjagt was drunk during the interview. "I'm out at my third Pro Bowl," he said, "I'm about to go in and throw a touchdown to Jerry Rice, we're honoring the Hall of Fame, and we're talking about our idiot kicker who got liquored up and ran his mouth off. The sad thing is he's a good kicker. He's a good kicker. But he's an idiot."[1]

The controversy eventually blew over, and the Colts got back to doing what they do best, winning games. They reached a high points in 2005 with a 14–2 campaign that included a dominant 26–7 victory against the Pittsburgh Steelers, the team they would face again in the second round of the playoffs.

For the Steelers, 2005 had not been a great follow-up to their impressive 15–1 season in 2004. Future Hall of Famer Jerome Bettis came back for one last attempt to win a Super Bowl championship, a title that never looked like it would happen after a three-game losing streak dropped them to 7–5. They found their stride at that point, winning their final four games to sneak into the playoffs, and then played a near-perfect second half in the opening round against Cincinnati, turning a 17–7 deficit into a 31–17 victory.

For as much momentum as their five-game winning streak had provided, it appeared likely that the streak and the season would end in Indianapolis. Still, head coach Bill Cowher and offensive coordinator Ken Whisenhunt came up with a strategy to catch the Colts off guard, and from the outset, it did exactly that.

With Indianapolis geared up to crush the potent Pittsburgh running game, Whisenhunt decided it was time to feature second-year quarterback Ben Roethlisberger. Consequently, the Colts were stunned when Roethlisberger threw on the first two plays of the game, the second resulting in a 36-yard completion to tight end Heath Miller. He completed six of seven passes on the drive, the last a six-yard scoring toss to Antwaan Randle El to give the Steelers a 7–0 lead.

The Pittsburgh defense was just as sharp, holding Manning and the Colts to no first downs in their first two series, giving the Steelers' offense a chance to shine once again. Roethlisberger continued his hot hand with a 45-yard completion to Hines Ward to the Indy 16 and then found Miller in the end zone as Pittsburgh had suddenly built a two-touchdown lead on the conference's No. 1 seed.

Things settled down a bit in the second quarter. With the Indianapolis defense finally slowing down the Steelers, Manning got rolling, directing the Colts on a 15-play, 96-yard drive that ate up over nine minutes of the clock. But the Steelers stood tall inside their own 10, forcing the Colts to settle for a field goal in what otherwise might have been a back-breaking turning point. The half ended with the Steelers still in command, 14–3.

The Steelers' defense continued to be aggressive, keeping the Colts off the board in the third quarter, while a 20-yard punt return by Randle El put the Steelers' offense in business again in Colts territory. Pittsburgh powered down to the one-yard line, where Bettis took the football into the end zone for what appeared to be the game-clinching touchdown with a little over a minute left in the third.

After the Steelers had contained him for most of the game, Manning finally came alive in the fourth quarter, starting with a 50-yard touchdown strike to Dallas Clark on the first play of the final stanza. A long Pittsburgh drive chewed up eight minutes of the clock but resulted in no points, and the Colts got cooking again on their ensuing possession. Pittsburgh safety Troy Polamalu appeared to seal victory with a diving interception, but officials ruled it an incomplete pass after Polamalu lost the football as he got up. Though replay review upheld the call, the NFL admitted the following week that the officials had made a mistake and it should have been ruled an interception. But that didn't matter. The Colts retained possession and capped the drive with a touchdown and two-point conversion to cut the lead to 21–18 with time running out.

The Indianapolis defense stuffed the Steelers, but the Pittsburgh defense then rose to the occasion, sacking Manning at his own two on fourth down to give the offense back the football with just over a minute to play. Once again, it appeared the Steelers had the game sealed up. Once again, this turned out not to be true.

On a handoff to Bettis, who rarely fumbled in his long career, he coughed up the ball, which was picked up by Nick Harper, a Colts defensive back who had been stabbed in the knee earlier in the week during a reported family dispute. Harper sprinted toward his end zone for the potential winning touchdown. With their goal-line offense out, the Steelers had very little speed on the field to catch up to Harper. If he made it to the clear, the Colts were headed to the Super Bowl. With the Steelers' AFC title hopes about to evaporate, a prone Roethlisberger stuck out his hand and tripped Harper at the Colts' 42.

It saved the game—for the moment. Manning still drove the Colts to the Pittsburgh 26, when they called on their "idiot" kicker to send the game to overtime. At the time, Vanderjagt was the most accurate kicker in NFL history, so tying the game seemed a sure thing. But once again, this game provided the unexpected. Incredibly, Vanderjagt missed badly to the right, and the Steelers were euphoric, celebrating their return trip to the AFC Championship.

The Colts were devastated, especially their beleaguered kicker. "It's extreme disbelief," Vanderjagt said. "From the Polamalu interception reversal to Jerome's fumble, everything seemed to be lined up in our favor."[2]

Everything except that final field goal attempt by the "idiot" kicker.

BOXSCORE

TEAM	1st	2nd	3rd	4th	FINAL
Pittsburgh	14	0	7	0	21
Indianapolis	0	3	0	15	18

TEAM	PLAY	SCORE
Pittsburgh	Randle El 6-yard pass from Roethlisberger (Reed kick)	7–0
Pittsburgh	Miller 7-yard pass from Roethlisberger (Reed kick)	14–0
Indianapolis	Vanderjagt 20-yard field goal	14–3
Pittsburgh	Bettis 1-yard run (Reed kick)	21–3
Indianapolis	Clark 50-yard pass from Manning (Vanderjagt kick)	21–10
Indianapolis	James 3-yard run (Wayne from Manning 2 points)	21–18

RUSHING

PITT	ATT	YDS	AVE	TD
Parker	17	59	3.5	0
Bettis	17	46	2.7	1
Haynes	2	8	4.0	0
Kreider	1	2	2.0	0
Roethlisberger	5	-3	-0.6	0

IND	ATT	YDS	AVE	TD
James	13	56	4.3	1
Rhodes	1	2	2.0	0

RECEIVING

PITT	REC	YDS	AVE	TD
Ward	3	68	22.7	0
Miller	3	61	20.3	1
Randle El	3	30	10.0	1
Parker	3	19	6.3	0
Tuman	1	19	19.0	0
Haynes	1	0	0.0	0

RECEIVING

IND	REC	YDS	AVE	TD
Wayne	7	97	13.9	0
James	5	26	5.2	0
Clark	4	84	21.0	1
Harrison	3	52	18.3	0
Fletcher	2	18	9.0	0
Stokley	1	13	13.0	0

PASSING

PITT	COMP	ATT	PCT	YDS	TD	INT
Roethlisberger	14	24	58.3	197	2	1

IND	COMP	ATT	PCT	YDS	TD	INT
Manning	22	38	57.9	290	1	0

STEELERS 36, CLEVELAND BROWNS 33
JANUARY 5, 2003

Epic Comeback

The 2002 Cleveland Browns appeared to be a young team on the rise as they came into Heinz Field for their first-round playoff matchup against the Pittsburgh Steelers. In only their fourth year of existence after being granted a new franchise in 1999 to replace the original that moved to Baltimore four years earlier, the Browns had seemingly turned the corner in the second half of the '02 season by winning five of their final seven contests to secure a wild-card spot in the playoffs.

But along the way to a 9–7 record, the Browns had lost twice to the division-champion Steelers, each by three points in tight contests. And if they hoped to avoid a three-game sweep, they'd have to do it without starting quarterback Tim Couch, who suffered a broken leg in the last game of the regular season. Couch was replaced by little-known Kelly Holcomb, a third-year quarterback from Middle Tennessee State who had started only three games prior to the playoff in Pittsburgh.

While inexperienced, Holcomb would at least have the advantage of throwing at a banged-up Steeler secondary who had suffered injuries late in the year. On the other side of the ball, the Steelers would also be starting Tommy Maddox, a quarterback with no playoff experience.

The feel-good story of 2002 was all about Maddox, who was coming off an MVP performance in the XFL—the one-year professional football league that was the brainchild of World Wrestling Entertainment boss Vince McMahon—when he was signed in 2001 by the Steelers. Formerly a first-round draft pick by the Denver Broncos, who hoped he would be the next John Elway, Maddox struggled and was out of the NFL four years later. But his second go-around was much more promising. He took over the starting job from Kordell Stewart in 2002 and led the Steelers to the AFC North Division crown, completing 62 percent of his passes for 2,836 yards and 20 touchdowns.

With both quarterbacks having no playoff experience, most expected it was going to be a defensive struggle. Right away, Holcomb defied expectations, connecting with wideout Kevin Johnson for an 83-yard pass on the game's third play, setting up a Cleveland touchdown and a quick 7–0 lead. The Browns added to their lead on the first play of the second quarter when Holcomb hit Dennis Northcutt for another scoring pass following a fumbled Pittsburgh punt return. The Steelers made up for their special-teams flub minutes later when Antwaan Randle El returned a punt 66 yards for a touchdown to cut the lead in half. The Browns tacked on a field goal, and the Steelers missed an opportunity to close out the half with points when Jeff Reed's 46-yard attempt sailed wide, maintaining Cleveland's 17–7 advantage.

The Steelers' hopes for a comeback dimmed further in the third quarter when Northcutt returned a punt 59 yards to the Pittsburgh 14 and then caught a Holcomb pass in the end zone moments later to make it 24–7. The Browns were then poised to put the nail in the coffin midway through the third quarter, driving into Pittsburgh territory on their next possession, but Mike Logan intercepted a Holcomb pass at the Pittsburgh 25 to halt the drive—and Cleveland's momentum.

With their chances fading, Maddox attacked the Browns' defense, aggressively completing seven passes on the next possession, the last to Plaxico Burress for a touchdown that cut the lead to 10 points.

The Browns' backup quarterback directed his offense on another scoring drive, ending with a field goal that made it 27–14 on the last play of the third quarter. After Holcomb had dominated the game for the first 45 minutes, Maddox would control the last 15.

He hit Randle El three times for 56 yards on the next drive and then connected with Jerame Tuman for a three-yard touchdown to cut the margin to six points. But Holcomb wasn't done just yet. He led the Browns downfield once more for another touchdown to push the lead to 33–21 with 10 minutes left.

After an exchange of punts, the Steelers took over at their own 23 with 5:30 to play, needing a touchdown to stay alive. Once again, Maddox delivered, fulfilling the leadership he'd demonstrated at halftime. "Tommy brought the whole team together at halftime and told us what we were going to do," wide receiver Terence Mathis said." He said, "If you don't think we're going to win this game, you need to go back into the locker room." It would really show in the last few minutes of the game, with a quick drive downfield aided by three

Cleveland penalties and capped by a touchdown toss to Hines Ward to cut the lead to five points with 3:11 remaining.[1]

Aided by three Browns penalties, including an unnecessary roughness call on Robert Griffith which put Pittsburgh inside the Cleveland 20, Maddox made the score 33–28 on a five-yard toss to Hines Ward with 3:11 left.

The Browns had an opportunity to melt the clock, but on third and 12, Northcutt dropped an easy catch that would have delivered a first down, and the Browns were forced to punt back to a hot Pittsburgh offense with 2:42 remaining.

Sixty-one yards away from a victory, Maddox sliced the vulnerable Browns' secondary. First came a 24-yard pass to Plaxico Burress, then a 10-yarder to Ward, followed by a 17-yard catch by Burress. A seven-yard toss to Ward pushed them to the Cleveland 3 with a minute left.

The stadium was now electric, as fans who only moments before saw no chance of a victory could now taste it. Their excitement turned into euphoria when fullback Chris Fuamatu-Ma'afala burst up the middle for the go-ahead touchdown. Randle El threw a pass to Tuman on a creative play call for the two-point conversion, and the Steelers had victory in their grasp with 54 seconds on the clock. Holcomb hurriedly tried to get the Browns into field-goal range, but time expired after a completion to the Pittsburgh 29. The Steelers had completed a remarkable comeback.

It had turned out to be one of the most memorable matchups in the history of the teams' long rivalry. They combined for 879 of offense, as both quarterbacks excelled in their first postseason action: Holcomb threw for 429 yards, and Maddox tossed for 367.

But for all the fireworks, the result was the same as the two gritty defensive battles the teams had endured in the regular season: a three-point Pittsburgh victory, only this one was defined by one of the greatest comebacks in playoff history. "This is going to hurt," a despondent Northcutt said afterward. "This burns inside. It's going to be very hard to move on."[2]

His words proved prophetic as the loss proved to be the end of the rapid ascent up the NFL standings for Cleveland. Instead of going to the next level, the franchise has floundered since never returning to the postseason. For the winners of this epic comeback, three years later they would become Super Bowl Champions as their never-say-die attitude truly served them well in the first decade of the twenty-first century.

BOXSCORE

TEAM	1st	2nd	3rd	4th	FINAL
Cleveland	7	10	7	9	33
Pittsburgh	0	7	7	22	36

TEAM	PLAY	SCORE
Cleveland	Green 1-yard run (Dawson kick)	7–0
Cleveland	Northcutt 32-yard pass from Holcomb (Dawson kick)	14–0
Pittsburgh	Randle El 66-yard punt return (Reed kick)	14–7
Cleveland	Dawson 31-yard field goal	17–7
Cleveland	Northcutt 15-yard pass from Holcomb (Dawson kick)	24–7
Pittsburgh	Burress 6-yard pass from Maddox (Reed kick)	24–14
Cleveland	Dawson 24-yard field goal	27–14
Pittsburgh	Tuman 3-yard pass from Maddox (Reed kick)	27–21
Cleveland	Davis 22-yard pass from Holcomb (Dawson kick)	33–21
Pittsburgh	Ward 5-yard pass from Maddox (Reed kick)	33–28
Pittsburgh	Fuamatu-Ma'afala 3-yard run (Reed kick)	33–36

RUSHING

PITT	ATT	YDS	AVE	TD
Zereoue	13	73	5.6	0
Maddox	2	7	3.5	0
Fuamatu-Ma'afala	2	4	2.0	1
Ward	1	4	4.0	0
Randle El	1	3	3.0	0
Bettis	1	-2	-2.0	0

RUSHING

CLEVE	ATT	YDS	AVE	TD
Green	25	30	1.2	1
Northcutt	1	5	5.0	0
Holcomb	2	3	1.5	0

RECEIVING

PITT	REC	YDS	AVE	TD
Ward	11	104	9.5	1
Burress	6	100	16.8	1
Randle El	5	85	17.0	0
Mathis	3	40	13.3	0
Tuman	3	18	6.0	1
Fuamatu-Ma'afala	2	20	10.0	0

CLEVE	REC	YDS	AVE	TD
Northcutt	6	92	15.3	2
White	5	45	9.0	0
Johnson	4	140	35.0	0
Campbell	3	31	10.3	0
Davis	2	65	32.5	1
Morgan	2	30	15.0	0
Green	2	8	4.0	0
King	1	16	16.0	0
Sanders	1	2	2.0	0

PASSING

PITT	COMP	ATT	PCT	YDS	TD	INT
Maddox	30	48	62.5	367	3	2

CLEVE	COMP	ATT	PCT	YDS	TD	INT
Holcomb	26	43	60.4	429	3	1

STEELERS 31, LOS ANGELES RAMS 19
JANUARY 20, 1980

City of Champions

In the long history of Major League Baseball and the National Football League, only twice had a city won world championships in both sports in the same year. In 1956, the New York Yankees and football Giants won their respective titles, as did the Baltimore Orioles and Colts in 1970.

After the Pittsburgh Pirates came back from a three-games-to-one deficit to capture the 1979 World Series against the Orioles, the Steelers had the opportunity to make Pittsburgh the third city to join this elite club. All they had to do was take care of business against the heavy underdog Los Angeles Rams in Super Bowl XIV.

On paper at least, the Rams were the weakest team ever to reach the Super Bowl. They'd stood at 5–6 in mid-November and had lost starting quarterback Pat Haden for the remainder of the season with a broken finger. In his absence, third-year signal-caller Vince Ferragamo guided them to four wins in their last five games to capture the NFC West title with a modest 9–7 record. Ferragamo saved his best for the playoffs, leading the Rams to upset victories over Dallas and Tampa Bay to pave the way to the NFC crown.

Though the game would be played in their own backyard at the Rose Bowl in Pasadena, the Rams entered their first Super Bowl as 10½-point underdogs against the vastly more experienced Steelers.

Pittsburgh, meanwhile, had experienced only modest turbulence en route to its fourth Super Bowl appearance in six years, going 12–4 to win the AFC Central before toppling Miami and Houston with relative ease in the playoffs. On paper, the game looked like a mismatch. But as the old saying goes, the games aren't played on paper.

It all started out innocently enough, with Pittsburgh stuffing the Rams on their first series and then driving 55 yards to set up a field goal to give the Steelers an early 3–0 lead midway through the first quarter. Then Ferragamo and running back Wendell Tyler, who led Los Angeles in rushing with 1,109 yards during the regular season, would show Pittsburgh that this would be no easy victory.

Tyler broke free for a 39-yard run to the Pittsburgh 14, and six plays later Cullen Bryan scored from a yard out to give the Rams a 7–3 lead. Aided by a 45-yard kickoff return by Larry Anderson—who would have a fantastic day in returns—the Steelers bounced right back, surging ahead again on a short Franco Harris scoring run minutes later.

Rather than folding after Pittsburgh's counterpunch, the Rams took control of the game and rode momentum into the half. Clutch completions by Ferragamo set up the game-tying field goal, and four minutes later, L.A.'s Dave Elmendorf intercepted an errant Terry Bradshaw, which led to another field goal, providing the Rams with a 13–10 advantage that lasted until the intermission. Halfway through, this was clearly not the Super Bowl America had been expecting.

Another long kickoff return by Anderson started the third quarter, and the Steelers' offense cashed in with an acrobatic 47-yard touchdown reception by Lynn Swann to put Pittsburgh back on top.

Once more, when it appeared the Rams might begin to fade, they would not be intimidated. On the ensuing drive, a 50-yard pass by Ferragamo propelled the Rams into Pittsburgh territory. Then on a halfback-option pass, veteran Lawrence McCutcheon connected with Ron Smith for a 24-yard touchdown to give the Rams the lead once again. The extra point was missed, but Los Angeles still carried a surprising 19–17 lead going into the game's final quarter.

It was a situation in which championship teams respond with big plays, and that's exactly what the Steelers did. On third and eight from his own 27, Bradshaw fired a long pass to a streaking John Stallworth, who'd blown past cornerback Rod Perry and pulled in the football for a 73-yard touchdown and a 24–19 Pittsburgh lead.

The Rams had one last push left in them. With the clock ticking down, they drove to the Pittsburgh 32, but Ferragamo was intercepted by Pittsburgh linebacker Jack Lambert at the Pittsburgh 14 to halt the momentum. Bradshaw and Co. then put the icing on the cake. A 45-yard toss to Stallworth and a pass-interference penalty on the Rams in the end zone set up the game-clinching one-yard touchdown by Harris with just under two minutes left. When the final seconds ticked down, the Steelers became the first team to win four Super

Bowls, and Pittsburgh became the third sports city to win both a World Series and a Super Bowl in the same sports calendar year.

The headline in the *Pittsburgh Post-Gazette* the next day read "Four Down, '80s to go." Of course there were no world championships in the 1980s—this was the last for this memorable team. But on this day they were the kings of the football world, as their enthusiastic fans marched on Market Square in the center of Pittsburgh to celebrate what this town had become: "The City of Champions."

BOXSCORE

TEAM	1st	2nd	3rd	4th	FINAL
Los Angeles	7	6	6	0	19
Pittsburgh	3	7	7	14	31

TEAM	PLAY	SCORE
Pittsburgh	Bahr 41-yard field goal	0–3
Los Angeles	Bryant 1-yard run (Corral kick)	7–3
Pittsburgh	Harris 1-yard run (Bahr kick)	7–10
Los Angeles	Corral 31-yard field goal	10–10
Los Angeles	Corral 45-yard field goal	13–10
Pittsburgh	Swann 47-yard pass from Bradshaw (Bahr kick)	13–17
Los Angeles	Smith 24-yard pass from McCutcheon (kick failed)	19–17
Pittsburgh	Stallworth 73-yard pass from Bradshaw (Bahr kick)	19–24
Pittsburgh	Harris 1-yard run (Bahr kick)	19–31

RUSHING

PITT	ATT	YDS	AVE	TD
Harris	20	46	2.3	2
Bleier	10	25	2.5	0
Bradshaw	3	9	3.0	0
Thornton	4	4	1.0	0

RUSHING

LA	ATT	YDS	AVE	TD
Tyler	17	60	3.5	0
Bryant	6	30	5.0	1
McCutcheon	5	10	2.0	0
Ferragamo	1	7	7.0	0

RECEIVING

PITT	REC	YDS	AVE	TD
Swann	5	79	15.8	1
Stallworth	3	121	40.3	1
Harris	3	66	22.0	0
Cunningham	2	21	10.5	0
Thornton	1	22	22.0	0

LA	REC	YDS	AVE	TD
Waddy	3	75	25.0	0
Bryant	3	21	7.0	0
Tyler	3	20	6.7	0
Dennard	2	32	16.0	0
Nelson	2	20	10.0	0
Smith	1	24	24.0	1
Hill	1	28	28.0	0
McCutcheon	1	16	16.0	0

PASSING

PITT	COMP	ATT	PCT	YDS	TD	INT
Bradshaw	14	21	66.7	309	2	3

LA	COMP	ATT	PCT	YDS	TD	INT
Ferragamo	15	25	60.0	212	0	1
McCutcheon	1	1	100.0	24	1	0

STEELERS 23, BALTIMORE RAVENS 14
JANUARY 18, 2009

Win One for the Home Team

Home-field advantage in the National Football League postseason is golden. It's the carrot at the end of the stick for those teams that fought hard during the regular season and posted the best records to get the best possible seeding going into the playoffs. And with those high seedings come home games.

Since the second renaissance of the Pittsburgh Steelers in the early 1990s through the 2007 season, they'd earned home-field advantage in the AFC Championship game five times. But remarkably, the home-field advantage hadn't paid off as expected, as the Steelers lost four of those five games. Each of those four defeats left a bitter taste in the Steelers' mouths, as they left the field knowing they were expected to get to the Super Bowl but hadn't delivered on their own home turf.

When the Steelers once again earned home-field advantage for the 2008 AFC Championship against their bitter rivals from Baltimore, all those horrible memories started to resurface. Mike Tomlin had replaced Bill Cowher as head coach the year before and was hell-bent on erasing those memories and winning one for the home crowd.

The AFC North rivals had already played two memorable games in 2008. The Steelers topped the visiting Ravens in overtime in September, then a late touchdown by Pittsburgh wideout Santonio Holmes gave Pittsburgh a narrow 13–9 victory in Baltimore to complete the sweep. Consequently, the Steelers edged Baltimore by a game for the division title, which allowed them to host the third encounter at Heinz Field.

Pittsburgh, facing one of the most difficult schedules in NFL history that included six opponents who qualified for the playoffs, had built a formidable defense that simply overwhelmed opposing offenses, allowing fewer points and total yards than any team in the NFL. If the Steelers were to snap their string of tough conference title game losses, the defense would have to lead them.

But it was the Pittsburgh offense that started strong. Sparked by a 45-yard completion to Hines Ward on the opening series, the Steelers quickly drove downfield and kicked a field goal for an early 3–0 lead. Five minutes later, it swelled to 6–0 following a Pittsburgh interception, and in the opening minutes, it was clear that the Steelers' defense was confusing rookie quarterback Joe Flacco. Still, the lead was just six points, and Pittsburgh fans knew it was missed opportunities like those that had haunted the team in previous AFC Championships.

On the second play of the second quarter, Roethlisberger hit Holmes for a 65-yard touchdown bomb that put Pittsburgh up 13–0. It was a play that the Steelers' quarterback would later admit didn't exactly come out of the playbook but was rather designed "just like on the playground."[1]

But the Ravens fought back. A long punt return moments later gave them possession at the Pittsburgh 17, and then a pass-interference penalty at the 3 dug them out of a third-down hole. Running back Willis McGahee took it the final yards for a touchdown, and suddenly a game that Pittsburgh had dominated was just 13–7 at the half.

Late in the third quarter, the Steelers pushed the lead to nine points with another field goal, but a poor Pittsburgh punt early in the fourth opened the door for the Ravens again. A rejuvenated Flacco suddenly looked like a veteran, leading Baltimore down the field on a drive that once again ended with a McGahee touchdown, this one from a yard out to bring the Ravens within two points with 9:32 left.

The fragile psyche of the Heinz Field crowd seemed to carry over to the Steelers, who promptly gave the ball back to Baltimore. Flacco picked up where he left off, completing a 20-yard pass for a first down, and it appeared the Steelers' fortunes in the AFC title game were going the way of their previous disappointments in 1994, 1997, 2001, and 2004.

But then a curly-haired savior saved the day. Safety Troy Polamalu leapt up to intercept a pass intended for Derrick Mason at the Baltimore 40 and then zigzagged through the stunned Ravens players for a touchdown that clinched the game and exorcised the Steelers' old ghosts.

The crowd instantly went from jittery to euphoric, while Flacco and the Ravens saw their Super Bowl dreams go up in smoke. The Baltimore rookie quarterback was dumbfounded. "I think Troy was probably just able to read my eyes," he said. "I think he was just able to jump over there, read a little bit and he made a nice play."[2]

Two plays later, whatever marginal chance the Ravens had for a comeback was laid to rest when Ryan Clark leveled McGahee following a completion, causing a fumble that Pittsburgh linebacker Lawrence Timmons scooped up.

The curse was now a thing of the past. What troubling memories the Steeler Nation had of AFC Championships past were now overrun with that of Polamalu's spectacular interception, a play that gave them the conference championship in front of the home crowd and a chance to finally leave the stadium with the conference championship trophy in hand.

BOXSCORE

TEAM	1ST	2ND	3RD	4TH	FINAL
Baltimore	0	7	0	7	14
Pittsburgh	6	7	3	7	23

TEAM	PLAY	SCORE
Pittsburgh	Reed 34-yard field goal	0–3
Pittsburgh	Reed 42-yard field goal	0–6
Pittsburgh	Holmes 65-yard pass from Roethlisberger (Reed kick)	0–13
Baltimore	McGahee 3-yard run (Stover kick)	7–13
Pittsburgh	Reed 46-yard field goal	7–16
Baltimore	McGahee 1-yard run (Stover kick)	14–16
Pittsburgh	Polamalu 40-yard interception return (Reed kick)	14–23

RUSHING

PITT	ATT	YDS	AVE	TD
Parker	24	47	2.0	0
Moore	1	6	6.0	0
Washington	1	1	1.0	0
Roethlisberger	2	-2	-1.0	0

RUSHING

BALT	ATT	YDS	AVE	TD
McGahee	20	60	3.0	2
Clayton	1	16	16.0	0
L. McClain	1	3	3.0	0
J. McClain	1	3	3.0	0
Rice	1	2	2.0	0
Flacco	2	-8	-4.0	0

RECEIVING

PITT	REC	YDS	AVE	TD
Miller	3	62	20.7	0
Ward	3	55	18.3	0
Washington	3	21	7.0	0
Holmes	2	70	35.0	1
Sweed	2	20	10.0	0
Moore	1	9	9.0	0
Parker	1	-2	-2.0	0

BALT	REC	YDS	AVE	TD
Rice	3	43	14.3	0
Mason	3	41	13.7	0
Heap	3	26	8.7	0
Clayton	2	18	9.0	0
McGahee	2	13	6.5	0

PASSING

PITT	COMP	ATT	PCT	YDS	TD	INT
Roethlisberger	16	33	48.5	255	1	0

BALT	COMP	ATT	PCT	YDS	TD	INT
Flacco	13	30	43.3	141	0	3

STEELERS 21, SEATTLE SEAHAWKS 10
FEBRUARY 6, 2006

One for the Thumb

When the Pittsburgh Steelers defeated the Los Angeles Rams in Super Bowl XIV, it gave them a record four Super Bowl championships. Wanting more, the battle cry from fans the following season became "one for the thumb"—a fifth ring.

When it didn't happen in 1980, the confident members of Steeler Nation simply assumed it would happen soon. The years began to pass quickly, and the careers of the Hall of Fame players began to wind down. By the mid-1980s, the team had been relegated to the bottom half of the AFC Central Division standings, and the assumption that there would someday be a fifth ring became a pipe dream.

Following their reemergence as an NFL power in the early 1990s, they had a chance to capture their fifth title in Super Bowl XXX but were stopped by the Dallas Cowboys, losing football's big game for the first time.

Over the next 10 years, the Steelers knocked on the door of a fifth championship but could never quite get there. The "one for the thumb" mantra was now a plea more than a demand. In 2005, amid unlikely circumstances, the Steelers sneaked into the postseason as the AFC's last seed and then won three straight road games to return to the Super Bowl. If they were to get that fifth ring, they would do so on the arm of their second-year quarterback Ben Roethlisberger.

Roethlisberger may have been in the league for only two seasons, but he had a remarkable 22–3 record as a starter and had led them to the AFC Championship the year before.

Roethlisberger was at his best in the 2005 postseason and hoped to carry his momentum into Super Bowl Sunday against the Seattle Seahawks at Ford Field in Detroit.

Adding even more significance to the game at Detroit's Ford Field was a homecoming of sorts for Pittsburgh running back Jerome Bettis, who'd grown up in the Motor City and now would close out his long career by playing in his first Super Bowl in his hometown.

With a large contingent of the crowd cheering for the Steelers at the game's outset, the Seahawks momentarily silenced them with an impressive drive downfield. They appeared to take a touchdown lead when Darrell Jackson caught a pass from quarterback Matt Hasselbeck in the end zone, but the officials caught Jackson making a slight push-off on Pittsburgh safety Chris Hope and penalized Jackson, wiping out the score. Seattle had to settle for a 47-yard field goal and a 3–0 lead as the first quarter ended.

Seattle's defense continued to confuse Roethlisberger through the opening minutes of the second quarter, and while the Steelers were being outplayed, they still only trailed by three as halftime approached. With just under five minutes left in the period, Roethlisberger connected with Hines Ward on a 40-yard bomb to the Seattle 3 on third and 28. Two plays later, on third and goal from the Seattle 1, Roethlisberger kept the ball and plowed forward, stretching out toward the end zone for an apparent touchdown. Though replays were inconclusive, the officials ruled it a touchdown, and replay review didn't overturn the call, giving the Steelers a 7–3 lead.

Pittsburgh's momentum carried over to the second half, when on the second play of the third quarter, running back Willie Parker followed a savage block by Alan Fanaca and sprinted downfield for a 75-yard touchdown, a Super Bowl record, which increased the Pittsburgh advantage to 11 points.

Following a missed field goal by the Seahawks—their second of the game—the Steelers embarked on their first sustained drive, led by Bettis, who was blasting holes in the Seattle front wall. The Steelers reached the Seattle 3, but then a Roethlisberger pass intended for Cedric Wilson was short and picked off by Seattle's Kelly Herndon, who returned it 76 yards to the Pittsburgh 20 to turn the game completely around. Two plays later, Hasselbeck found Jerramy Stevens for a touchdown, and instead of a 21–3 Pittsburgh lead, it was now 14–10 with the momentum now firmly in Seattle's corner.

The Seahawks were poised to take control of the game early in the fourth quarter after driving to the Pittsburgh 19, and then a completed pass appeared to set up first and goal from the 3. But the Steelers caught another break when Seattle was penalized for holding, wiping out the play. Two snaps later, Hasselbeck overthrew his receiver, and Pittsburgh cornerback Ike Taylor picked off the pass.

Three plays after that, the Steelers finally put the nail in the Seahawks' coffin. On a trick play, Roethlisberger tossed a lateral to receiver Antwaan Randle El, who rolled to his right, broke free on a block by Roethlisberger, and then tossed a perfect pass downfield to Ward, who sprinted into the end zone to complete a 43-yard touchdown that made it 21–10 with nine minutes to play.

As the clock hit zero, several dreams were now being realized. Bettis had come home to Detroit to finally win his long-awaited championship and then promptly retired on the presentation stand proudly holding the Lombardi Trophy. Head Coach Bill Cowher, who had been so close so many times, only to fall short of this moment, finally had a Super Bowl to call his own. Finally and most importantly, the franchise had their "one for the thumb."

BOXSCORE

TEAM	1st	2nd	3rd	4th	FINAL
Seattle	3	0	7	0	10
Pittsburgh	0	7	7	7	21

TEAM	PLAY	SCORE
Seattle	Brown 47-yard field goal	3–0
Pittsburgh	Roethlisberger 1-yard run (Reed kick)	3–7
Pittsburgh	Parker 75-yard run (Reed kick)	3–14
Seattle	Stevens 16-yard pass from Hasselbeck (Brown kick)	10–14
Pittsburgh	Ward 43-yard pass from Randle El (Reed kick)	10–21

RUSHING

PITT	ATT	YDS	AVE	TD
Parker	10	93	9.3	1
Bettis	14	43	3.1	0
Roethlisberger	7	25	3.6	1
Ward	1	18	18.0	0
Hatnes	1	2	2.0	0

SEA	ATT	YDS	AVE	TD
Alexander	20	95	4.8	0
Hasselbeck	3	35	11.7	0
Strong	2	7	3.5	0

RECEIVING

PITT	REC	YDS	AVE	TD
Ward	5	123	24.6	1
Randle El	3	22	7.3	0
Wilson	1	20	20.0	0
Parker	1	1	1.0	0

SEA	REC	YDS	AVE	TD
Engram	6	70	11.7	0
Jurevicius	5	93	18.6	0
Jackson	5	50	10.0	0
Stevens	3	25	8.3	1
Strong	2	15	7.5	0
Hannam	2	12	6.0	0
Alexander	2	2	1.0	0
Morris	1	6	6.0	0

PASSING

PITT	COMP	ATT	PCT	YDS	TD	INT
Roethlisberger	9	21	42.9	123	0	2
Randle El	1	1	100.00	43	1	0

SEA	COMP	ATT	PCT	YDS	TD	INT
Hasselbeck	26	49	53.1	273	1	1

Over the Hump

In their first 42 seasons, playoff appearances had been rare, but league championship appearances had been nil. Twice before they'd stood on the doorstep, a win away from a title game in both 1947 and 1972, only to be turned away.

Two years after their second defeat, they would get a third opportunity, this time against the Oakland Raiders in one of the toughest stadiums in football: the Oakland-Alameda Coliseum.

It had been a strange year for the Steelers, one that began with a quarterback controversy between Joe Gilliam and Terry Bradshaw. After Gilliam led the Steelers to a 4–1–1 start but then started struggling, Bradshaw took over, directing the Steelers the rest of the way to the AFC Central Division crown. Pittsburgh then coasted to an easy victory over Buffalo in a divisional playoff and into the AFC Championship against the Raiders, a team that had humiliated them in their previous two meetings, including a 17–0 win in Pittsburgh earlier in the 1974 season. The Raiders had won the AFC West with a 12–2 record and fully expected to get back to the Super Bowl for the first time in seven years.

Early on, it looked like the Raiders would continue their dominance over Pittsburgh. A fumble on a punt return by Pittsburgh wideout Lynn Swann—part of a remarkable group of Steelers rookies in '74—set up an Oakland field goal by 47-year-old kicker George Blanda to put the Raiders ahead 3–0.

The Steelers were poised to tie the game late in the first quarter, but Roy Gerela missed a chip-shot 20-yard field goal. He bounced back to make a 23-yard attempt six minutes later, and by now the Steelers had firmly grasped the game's momentum. Unfortunately, they were unable to cash it in for points. Just before the half, a promising drive to the Oakland 10 ended when

Bradshaw was intercepted, and the Raiders scurried downfield in the moments before the intermission. On the brink of taking back the lead, the Raiders saw the opportunity slip through their fingers when Pittsburgh linebacker Jack Lambert—another talented rookie—broke through to block Blanda's field-goal attempt and preserve the 3–3 tie.

Despite controlling the game for much of the first half, the Steelers appeared to run out of gas early in the third quarter when Oakland quarterback Ken Stabler drove his offense 80 yards, capping it off with a 38-yard touchdown pass to Cliff Branch. It appeared the Steelers were on their way to another playoff defeat.

At that point the potent Pittsburgh running game sprang to life. Franco Harris burst through for a 16-yard gain, then Rocky Bleier picked up 35 to push the Steelers into scoring territory. Moments later, Harris tied the game again with an eight-yard scoring run early in the fourth quarter.

With a championship at stake, the Pittsburgh defense rose to the occasion. Holding the Raiders to just 29 rushing yards for the game, the Steelers continually thwarted Oakland's offense with the game on the line. Linebacker Jack Ham picked off his second pass of the game to put the Steelers in business again. Moments later, on third-and-goal from the Oakland six, Swann made up for his earlier fumble by grabbing a six-yard touchdown pass to give the Steelers their first lead of the day at 17–10.

The Raiders made one final push, as Stabler completed a 42-yard pass to Branch, but again the Steel Curtain defense strengthened, forcing Oakland to settle for a field goal to cut the lead to four points with just under eight minutes to play.

Both defenses stood tall over the next few minutes, and with just under two minutes left, the Raiders regained possession for one final chance. Once again, the Steelers' defense came up with the big play when cornerback J. T. Thomas intercepted a Stabler pass at the Pittsburgh 39 and returned it to the Oakland 24 with time running out. A couple of plays later, Harris blasted through a beaten Oakland defense for a 21-yard touchdown that put the icing on the cake of a 24–13 victory. After more than four decades of failure, the Pittsburgh Steelers were headed to the Super Bowl.

"We're a completely different team now," Bleier said after the game. "In the past we looked for weaknesses and attacked from there, now we depend on our strengths and not other people's weaknesses. That's what a little confidence and maturity will do for you."[1]

That right mix had finally ended 42 years of disappointment, especially for owner Art Rooney. "Nobody loses harder than I do," Rooney had said so many times in the past, "but nobody knows it because I don't show it." He wouldn't have to worry about not showing it on this day. In true Rooney style, he didn't brag or gloat but just took the win in stride with the same demeanor as always.[2]

But the tears in his eyes showed what he felt on the inside, knowing his team would finally play for an NFL championship.

BOXSCORE

TEAM	1st	2nd	3rd	4th	FINAL
Pittsburgh	0	3	0	21	24
Oakland	3	0	7	3	13

TEAM	PLAY	SCORE
Oakland	Blanda 40-yard field goal	0–3
Pittsburgh	Gerela 23-yard field goal	3–3
Oakland	Branch 38-yard pass from Stabler (Blanda kick)	3–10
Pittsburgh	Harris 8-yard run (Gerela kick)	10–10
Pittsburgh	Swann 6-yard pass from Bradshaw (Gerela kick)	17–10
Oakland	Blanda 24-yard field goal	17–13
Pittsburgh	Harris 21-yard run (Gerela kick)	24–13

RUSHING

PITT	ATT	YDS	AVE	TD
Harris	29	111	3.8	2
Bleier	18	98	5.4	0
Bradshaw	4	1	0.3	0

OAK	ATT	YDS	AVE	TD
Davis	10	16	1.6	0
Banaszak	3	7	2.3	0
Hubbard	7	6	0.9	0
Stabler	1	0	0.0	0

RECEIVING

PITT	REC	YDS	AVE	TD
Brown	2	37	18.5	0
Bleier	2	25	12.5	0
Swann	2	17	8.5	1
Stallworth	2	16	8.0	0

OAK	REC	YDS	AVE	TD
Branch	9	186	20.7	1
Moore	4	32	8.0	0
Biletnikoff	3	45	15.0	0
Davis	2	8	4.0	0
Banaszak	1	0	0.0	0

PASSING

PITT	COMP	ATT	PCT	YDS	TD	INT
Bradshaw	8	17	47.1	95	1	1

OAK	COMP	ATT	PCT	YDS	TD	INT
Stabler	19	36	52.7	271	1	3

STEELERS 20, INDIANAPOLIS COLTS 16
JANUARY 14, 1996

Redemption

It had been almost a year to the day that the Pittsburgh Steelers and their loyal fans suffered through one of the worst nightmares in franchise history. Playing the heavy-underdog San Diego Chargers in the 1994 AFC Championship game at Three Rivers Stadium, the Steelers squandered a 10-point third-quarter lead to fall behind by four in the final period, then lost the game when a fourth-down Pittsburgh pass from the San Diego 3 was knocked away with a minute remaining. Despite being outgained by nearly 200 total yards, the Chargers had defeated the Steelers and would represent the AFC in the Super Bowl.

It was a miserable end to what had been such a fantastic season. A year later the Steelers would get a chance for redemption as they once again marched to the conference title game. As they had the year before, they'd host the contest, this time against the upstart Indianapolis Colts, who'd barely qualified for the playoffs with a 9–7 record. They tripped up the Chargers in San Diego in the second round and then stunned the top-seeded Kansas City Chiefs to move to the brink of the Super Bowl.

The Steelers, of course, were a huge favorite against the Colts and were expected to ride their new offensive philosophy to Super Sunday. Running back Barry Foster, who'd set the all-time franchise record for rushing yards in a season in 1992 and had accumulated 3,943 yards in his career, had been traded to Carolina before the 1995 campaign began and then was cut by the Panthers. Switching gears from a power running attack, head coach Bill Cowher decided to feature quarterback Neil O'Donnell and the passing game in '95. The results were astounding. They went from 23rd in the NFL in passing in 1994 to eighth, and after a shaky 3–4 start, the new offense paved the way to eight victories in their last nine games and a playoff victory over Buffalo.

Though it had all the makings of an easy Pittsburgh victory, the game unfolded much like the previous year's championship.

The 11-point underdogs went ahead early after defensive tackle Tony Siragusa deflected an O'Donnell pass into the hands of linebacker Jeff Herrod, who returned the ball to the Pittsburgh 24. Four plays later, the Colts kicked a field goal for a 3–0 lead. Pittsburgh tied the contest before the opening period ended, but quarterback Jim Harbaugh directed the Colts on a long drive capped by another field goal to take the lead right back.

As the first half was winding down, thoughts of a year ago began to emerge in the minds of Steelers fans. Indianapolis was proving much tougher than anyone thought, but Pittsburgh began to pick up momentum on a long drive late in the second quarter. With under 30 seconds left, Pittsburgh reached the Indianapolis 5, then versatile rookie quarterback Kordell Stewart, who'd earned the nickname "Slash" during his debut season for his running, receiving, and throwing abilities, was inserted at receiver and caught a touchdown pass from O'Donnell to put Pittsburgh ahead, 10–6. Replays seemed to show Stewart had stepped out of bounds before getting both feet down in the end zone, but the touchdown stood.

The teams traded field goals in the third quarter, setting the stage for a memorable finish. The similarity to the 1994 AFC Championship then became eerie when Harbaugh tossed a long touchdown pass to wideout Floyd Turner, who'd broken free behind defensive back Darren Perry to put the Colts ahead 16–13 with less than nine minutes left. For the Steelers and their fans, it felt like 1994 all over again. "It was in the back of your mind," defensive lineman Ray Seals admitted after the game.[1]

Pittsburgh was unable to move the ball on the next series and punted back to the Colts, who then faced third and one deep in their own territory with less than four minutes remaining. On one of the critical plays of the game, Pittsburgh cornerback Willie Williams stuffed Warren short of the first down, and the Colts were forced to punt.

The Steelers took over at their own 33, and O'Donnell quickly moved them upfield. Pittsburgh wideout Ernie Mills made a critical clutch play when he knocked the football out of the grasp of Colts linebacker Quentin Coryatt on what appeared to be an interception, allowing the Steelers to keep the football. O'Donnell then completed a critical fourth-and-three pass to Andre Hastings for a first down and connected with Mills on a 37-yard strike that gave the Steelers a first down at the Indianapolis 1. Fullback Bam Morris took it the final three feet, and the Steelers had taken the lead back at 20–16 with just over a minute left.

Unfortunately for Pittsburgh, the underdog Colts weren't done. Harbaugh quickly drove them to the Pittsburgh 29 with time for just one more play. Harbaugh lofted a pass into the end zone, and it spiraled downward into a sea of hands as 61,000 fans watched with held breath. Perry tipped it, and the ball bounced backward, toward Colts receiver Aaron Bailey on the ground. The football landed in his lap, and for a moment it appeared the Steelers had just been denied a Super Bowl ticket once again. But what appeared like a dramatic Hail Mary completion fell harmlessly to the ground and was ruled incomplete as Three Rivers Stadium erupted in jubilation.

"Maybe it was poetic justice" an emotional Cowher exclaimed after the game. It certainly was as the fans were joyous, looking at a beleaguered opponent on the field instead of their own beloved Steelers losing another heartbreaker. It was true redemption for Pittsburgh and a trip to the Super Bowl for the first time in 16 years. While two weeks later their quest for a fifth Super Bowl title ended up squashed in the dust of the Arizona desert, on this day they were on the top of hill, inches away from what could have been a disaster that ended as one of the greatest victories in the franchise's history.[2]

BOXSCORE

TEAM	1st	2nd	3rd	4th	FINAL
Indianapolis	3	3	3	7	16
Pittsburgh	3	7	3	7	20

TEAM	PLAY	SCORE
Indianapolis	Blanchard 34-yard field goal	3–0
Pittsburgh	Johnson 31-yard field goal	3–3
Indianapolis	Blanchard 36-yard field goal	6–3
Pittsburgh	Stewart 5-yard pass from O'Donnell (Johnson kick)	6–10
Indianapolis	Blanchard 37-yard field goal	9–10
Pittsburgh	Johnson 36-yard field goal	9–13
Indianapolis	Turner 47-yard pass from Harbaugh (Blanchard kick)	16–13
Pittsburgh	Morris 1-yard run (Johnson kick)	16–20

RUSHING

PITT	ATT	YDS	AVE	TD
Pegram	10	46	4.6	0
Stewart	4	12	3.0	0
Morris	7	9	1.3	1
Williams	1	6	6.0	0
Mills	1	5	5.0	0
O'Donnell	1	2	2.0	0

IND	ATT	YDS	AVE	TD
Warren	15	53	3.5	0
Harbaugh	6	29	4.8	0
Crockett	1	2	2.0	0
Humphrey	1	-1	-1.0	0

RECEIVING

PITT	REC	YDS	AVE	TD
Thigpen	6	65	10.8	0
Williams	4	21	5.3	0
Morris	4	11	2.8	0
Mills	3	52	17.3	0
Hastings	3	21	7.0	0
Stewart	2	18	9.9	1
Holliday	1	8	8.0	0
Bruener	1	6	6.0	0
Pegram	1	3	3.0	0

IND	REC	YDS	AVE	TD
Dawkins	7	96	13.7	0
Warren	7	37	5.3	0
Turner	2	55	27.5	1
Crockett	2	22	11.0	0
Dilger	1	30	30.0	0
Stablein	1	18	18.0	0
Bailey	1	9	9.0	0

PASSING

PITT	COMP	ATT	PCT	YDS	TD	INT
O'Donnell	25	41	61.0	205	1	1

IND	COMP	ATT	PCT	YDS	TD	INT
Harbaugh	21	33	63.6	267	1	0
Warren	0	1	00.0	0	0	0

Baryshnikov in Cleats

Jerry Rice, perhaps the greatest wide receiver ever to step on the gridiron, modeled his entire Hall of Fame career on the greatest pass catcher in Pittsburgh Steelers history. "Lynn Swann was an idol," Rice said. "It would amaze me how he could fly through the air and make those catches. I'll never forget the one versus Dallas. It was the greatest catch I've ever seen."[1]

Most football fans are familiar with the catch Rice was referring to. But in reality, Swann made three spectacular catches in that Super Bowl, three of the most incredible acrobatic catches any NFL receiver had ever made, and he'd done it on the sport's biggest stage. That game—and those three catches—launched the second-year receiver from a potentially great pass catcher to one of the game's elite.

Swann was a unique athlete. Selected by the Steelers in the first round of the 1974 draft out of Southern California, he took a different approach to training. From the age of four, he trained in dance, concentrating on tap and ballet. With his graceful receptions, it didn't take long for him to earn the nickname "Baryshnikov in Cleats." Still, as his second season came to a close, most of the nation hadn't seen what Swann was capable of. They'd get their chance on 1976's Super Bowl Sunday.

After getting knocked unconscious and being carted off the field in the AFC title game two weeks earlier, there was some doubt about whether Swann would play in the Super Bowl against Dallas. Swann himself did not think he would be able to play after a concussion of that severity. Doctors left it up to him, but he was not sharp in practice and wasn't confident he'd be able to perform at his peak level. Ironically, Dallas defensive back Cliff Harris may have made his decision for him. As one of the leaders of a very physical Cowboys defense,

Harris predicted a rough game. "I'm not going to hurt anyone intentionally," he said, "but getting hit again must be in the back of Lynn Swann's mind." The quote angered Swann and motivated him. He decided to suit up.[2]

As prepared as the Steelers were, they were surprised by a reverse on the opening kickoff by Dallas's Thomas Henderson, who took the ball 48 yards to the Steeler 44. Though the long return didn't result in any points, the Cowboys caught another break five minutes later when Pittsburgh punter Bobby Walden fumbled the snap on his own 29, and Dallas recovered. On the next play, Steelers safety Mike Wagner thought he saw a particular play coming so he tried to alert his teammates. Unsure they heard him, he just backed up, hoping he could contain it. Dallas receiver Drew Pearson found an opening across the middle where Wagner had vacated and caught a pass from Roger Staubach for a touchdown. Pearson's catch would be overshadowed by another moments later.

From the Dallas 48, Terry Bradshaw launched a long pass to Swann, who was tightly covered by Mark Washington and Cliff Harris, the man who had inadvertently inspired Swann to play. Swann leapt over both defenders to catch the ball and somehow get his feet down in bounds at the Dallas 19 for an amazing catch. It set up the tying touchdown moments later as Bradshaw found tight end Randy Grossman for a score.

Dallas rebounded with a long drive powered by running back Robert Newhouse that set up a field goal to give the Cowboys a 10–7 lead early in the second quarter.

With less than four minutes left in the half and Pittsburgh stuck at its own 6, Bradshaw once again showed off his strong arm and heaved a pass down the center of the field toward Swann, who looked like he had absolutely no chance to catch what appeared to be an errant pass. Once again perfectly covered by Washington, Swann used his athleticism and ballet techniques to leap up just enough to knock the ball out of Washington's hands. As it bounced into the air, and the two players tumbled to the turf, Swann somehow maintained his concentration on the tipped ball, grabbing it on his knees at the Dallas 44 for a 50-yard gain in what remains one of the most breathtaking plays in Super Bowl history. Even though kicker Roy Gerela, who badly hurt his ribs on the opening kickoff, missed a 36-yard field goal as time was running out in the half, and the Steelers still trailed, Swann's catch seemed to have changed the game's momentum.

Early in the second half the Steel Curtain began to take control of the game. An interception by J. T. Thomas went for naught as the banged-up Gerela missed another field goal. The antagonistic Cliff Harris stopped in front of a dejected Gerela and taunted him by slapping his helmet. Pittsburgh linebacker Jack Lambert, who was blocking on the play and had already developed a reputation as one of the league's meanest players, grabbed Harris and flipped him violently to the ground. Harris got up, pointed at Lambert, but walked away. The Cowboys were still winning, but the Steelers had taken control.

The Cowboys nursed their narrow lead into the fourth quarter, but then Pittsburgh's Reggie Harrison broke through the line to block a Dallas punt. The ball sailed out of the end zone for a safety, and the Steelers had pulled within a point. On the ensuing possession, the Steelers drove to the Dallas 20, where Gerela finally came through with a field goal to give the Steelers a 12–10 lead with just under nine minutes remaining.

On the next play from scrimmage, Staubach fired a pass for Pearson from his own 15, the same pattern that earlier worked for a touchdown. This time Wagner read the play properly and picked it off, returning it to the Dallas 6. Gerela delivered once again to make it a five-point Pittsburgh edge.

When the Steelers got the ball back, they once again turned to their Baryshnikov in Cleats. From his own 36, Bradshaw tossed another long pass to Swann, but this one required no acrobatics. He caught it in stride at the Dallas 7 and strode into the end zone for a touchdown to make it 21–10. On the play Larry Cole crushed Bradshaw, who was knocked senseless and never saw Swann's catch.

The Cowboys weren't done. Moments later, Staubach hit Percy Howard for a 34-yard touchdown to bring Dallas to within four. When Pittsburgh was unable to move the ball under backup quarterback Terry Hanratty, who'd replaced Bradshaw after the vicious hit, Chuck Noll made the daring decision to go for it on fourth and one. The Dallas defense held, and Staubach and Co. took over with time running out. Out of time-outs, the Cowboys drove to the Pittsburgh 39 with just over a minute left; then Pittsburgh safety Glen Edwards intercepted a long pass in the end zone to secure the Steelers' second straight Super Bowl championship.

While the Pittsburgh defense had an incredible day, it was Lynn Swann who stole the show. His four receptions for 161 yards were enough to earn him Super Bowl MVP honors—marking the first time a receiver had earned the distinction. He showed that dance and football can coexist, paving the way for a generation of athletic receivers like Jerry Rice who wanted nothing more than to emulate the swanlike Lynn Swann.

BOXSCORE

TEAM	1st	2nd	3rd	4th	FINAL
Dallas	7	3	0	7	17
Pittsburgh	7	0	0	14	21

TEAM	PLAY	SCORE
Dallas	Pearson 29-yard pass from Staubach (Fritsch kick)	7–0
Pittsburgh	Grossman 7-yard pass from Bradshaw (Gerela kick)	7–7
Dallas	Fritsch 36-yard field goal	10–7
Pittsburgh	Harrison safety on blocked punt	10–9
Pittsburgh	Gerela 36-yard field goal	10–12
Pittsburgh	Gerela 18-yard field goal	10–15
Pittsburgh	Swann 64-yard pass from Bradshaw (kick failed)	10–21
Dallas	Howard 34-yard pass from Staubach (Fritsch kick)	17–21

RUSHING

PITT	ATT	YDS	AVE	TD
Harris	27	82	3.0	0
Bleier	15	51	3.4	0
Bradshaw	4	16	4.0	0

DAL	ATT	YDS	AVE	TD
Newhouse	16	56	3.5	0
Staubach	5	22	4.4	0
Dennison	5	16	3.2	0
Pearson	5	14	2.8	0

RECEIVING

PITT	REC	YDS	AVE	TD
Swann	4	161	40.3	1
Stallworth	2	8	4.0	0
Harris	1	26	26.0	0
Grossman	1	7	7.0	1
Brown	1	7	7.0	0

DALL	REC	YDS	AVE	TD
P. Pearson	5	53	10.6	0
Young	3	31	10.3	0
D. Pearson	2	59	29.5	1
Newhouse	2	12	6.0	0
Howard	1	34	34.0	1
Fugett	1	9	9.0	0
Dennison	1	6	6.0	0

PASSING

PITT	COMP	ATT	PCT	YDS	TD	INT
Bradshaw	9	19	47.3	209	2	0

DAL	COMP	ATT	PCT	YDS	TD	INT
Staubach	15	24	62.5	204	2	3

STEELERS 16, MINNESOTA VIKINGS 6
JANUARY 12, 1975

14,723 Days

In the early 1930s, Pittsburgh's own Art Rooney decided to buy a National Football League franchise for his hometown after the state of Pennsylvania voted to lift part of the blue laws that had prohibited commercial entertainment on Sundays, the day the NFL played most of its games. Little did anyone know at the time, it was the beginning of the franchise that would go on to win more Super Bowl championships than any other NFL squad.

But they were not successful at the beginning. They struggled through the 1930s and, outside of a single playoff appearance in 1947, the Steelers were a mainstay at the bottom of the standings for the first four decades of their existence. Players and coaches came and went. The only constant was that the Steelers were among the doormats of the league.

Things turned around quickly in the 1970s, and in 1974 the Steelers had finally gotten over the hump, capturing their first conference title and playing in Super Bowl IX. It had been 14,723 days since the team's first game, and long-suffering fans dreamed that 14,724 would be the day when the entire nation would finally look at this franchise differently, as champions instead of lovable losers.

While satisfying, it hadn't been a dream season to this point. A nasty quarterback controversy swirled around the team at the beginning of the season, and the offense struggled for much of the season, depending on a dominant defense to bail it out. On top of everything else, the Steelers would have their work cut out for them, facing the powerful Minnesota Vikings who, unlike the Steelers, had been successful almost from their outset, reaching three Super Bowls in their first 14 seasons.

This Super Bowl was intended to be the initial contest played at America's new wonder stadium, the Superdome in New Orleans, but construction was not complete, so the game was moved to nearby Tulane Stadium. Instead of a climate-controlled 70-degree temperature at kickoff, the two teams played on rain-soaked turf on an unusually cold New Orleans day.

The conditions were particularly troubling for Dwight White, one of the stalwarts of the Pittsburgh defense, who had come down with pneumonia earlier in the week and had dropped nearly 20 pounds by game time. White didn't want to miss out on the biggest day in the franchise's history, so despite the ravaging his body had endured, he suited up and, as it turned out, would play the game of his life.

Not surprisingly, the defenses took center stage, and the two punters became the center of attention as neither offense could get anything going. The Steelers had a chance to take a lead late in the first quarter with good field position after a short Minnesota punt, but Roy Gerela missed a field goal to keep the game scoreless. Another field-goal attempt went awry minutes later when holder Bobby Walden dropped the snap from center, and Steelers fans saw another scoring opportunity slip away. Minnesota returned the favor early in the second quarter, missing a short field goal after recovering a Rocky Bleier fumble at the Pittsburgh 22.

It seemed only appropriate that the Pittsburgh defense broke the deadlock midway through the second quarter. Minnesota quarterback Fran Tarkenton fumbled the snap at the Vikings' 10. The ball rolled into the end zone, where Tarkenton pounced on it, and Dwight White—who'd been in the hospital only days before—smothered Tarkenton for a safety, the first points in Super Bowl IX. The unusual 2–0 score held up until the half.

The Steelers caught another break on the opening kickoff of the third quarter when Marv Kellum recovered a Vikings fumble, giving Pittsburgh outstanding field position on the Minnesota 30. The Pittsburgh offensive line then overpowered the Minnesota front wall, opening massive holes for Franco Harris, who ripped off a 24-yard run and then a nine-yard sweep around left end and into the end zone to put Pittsburgh ahead 9–0.

The Steel Curtain defense continued to thwart Tarkenton and the Vikings, and it appeared the nine-point advantage was safe. Then, with a little over 10 minutes left in the game, Minnesota's Matt Blair broke through the Pittsburgh punt protection and blocked Walden's punt. The Vikings' Terry Brown recovered the ball in the end zone for a touchdown, and, though the ensuing extra point was missed, all of a sudden the Vikings were only down three, after getting thoroughly beaten throughout this game. Pittsburgh fans groaned, wondering if this day would go the way of most of the 14,000 before it.

This was a different Pittsburgh team. Just when they needed it most, after a season of adversity, the Steelers' offense put together a long clutch drive downfield. After Bradshaw hit tight end Larry Brown for 30 yards on a crucial third-and-two play, Bleier and Harris, who set a Super Bowl record with 158 rushing yards, ripped through the Minnesota defense, marching to the Vikings' 4 with just over three minutes left.

On third and goal, Joe Gilliam, who had taken over as quarterback from Bradshaw to start this campaign only to be relegated to backup duties midway through the season, suggested a pass play to Bradshaw and Noll. Bradshaw rolled to his right and threw a quick pass that found Brown in the back of the end zone. Brown was hit hard just as he caught the ball, but he hung on for the touchdown that gave the Steelers an insurmountable 16–6 lead and wiped away 42 years of frustration.

As the final seconds ticked down, many longtime members of the franchise broke into tears. The joy they never thought would come finally was here. In the locker room, Rooney accepted the Lombardi Trophy from NFL commissioner Pete Rozelle. Even in this moment of triumph, Rooney felt uncomfortable and felt his son Dan, who had taken over most of the team's day-to-day operations, should have accepted the trophy.

But for as much an impact as Dan had on building this championship team, it was only appropriate that Art Rooney stood on this stage. Full of emotion, he saw his thick glasses fogging up and was unable to speak, accepting the honor that for 14,723 days had eluded him.

On day number 14,724, his frustrations—and those of his loyal fan base—were finally over.

BOXSCORE

TEAM	1st	2nd	3rd	4th	FINAL
Pittsburgh	0	2	7	7	16
Minnesota	0	0	0	6	6

TEAM	PLAY	SCORE
Pittsburgh	White tackles Tarkenton in the end zone for a safety	2–0
Pittsburgh	Harris 9-yard run (Gerela kick)	9–0
Minnesota	T. Brown falls on block punt in end zone (Cox kick)	9–6
Pittsburgh	L. Brown 4-yard pass from Bradshaw (Gerela kick)	16–6

RUSHING

PITT	ATT	YDS	AVE	TD
Harris	34	158	4.6	1
Bleier	17	65	3.8	0
Bradshaw	5	33	6.6	0
Swann	1	-7	-7.0	0

MINN	ATT	YDS	AVE	TD
Foreman	12	18	1.5	0
Tarkenton	1	0	0.0	0
Osborn	8	-1	-0.1	0

RECEIVING

PITT	REC	YDS	AVE	TD
Brown	3	49	16.3	1
Stallworth	3	24	8.0	0
Bleier	2	11	5.5	0
Lewis	1	12	12.0	0

MINN	REC	YDS	AVE	TD
Foreman	5	50	10.0	0
Voigt	2	31	15.5	0
Osborn	2	7	3.5	0
Gilliam	1	16	16.0	0
Reed	1	-2	-2.0	0

PASSING

PITT	COMP	ATT	PCT	YDS	TD	INT
Bradshaw	9	14	64.3	96	1	0

MINN	COMP	ATT	PCT	YDS	TD	INT
Tarkenton	11	26	42.3	102	0	3

STEELERS 35, DALLAS COWBOYS 31
JANUARY 21, 1979

C-A-T

For much of Terry Bradshaw's career, he was often ridiculed. And not possessing much calm or cool in his early days in the NFL, he was also the target of criticism. He had a southern drawl, often spoke his mind, and was sometimes unfairly mocked for being less than intelligent. What's more, he showed an uncommon sensitivity that had many questioning whether he could take the pressure of NFL football.

While he would show glimpses of the talent the Steelers saw in him when they made him the first overall pick in the 1970 NFL draft, too often he would try to force passes where they shouldn't have been and would make decisions that kept Pittsburgh toward the bottom of the standings in the first few years of his career. He began to come into his own in 1974, bouncing back from an early season benching to lead the Steelers to their first Super Bowl title. By 1978 Bradshaw was on the top of the world. He'd directed Pittsburgh to a 14–2 record and a third Super Bowl appearance in five years with relative ease. Bradshaw led the league with 28 touchdown tosses and was named the National Football League's Most Valuable Player.

His career was seemingly at the zenith when the Steelers met the Dallas Cowboys in Super Bowl XIII. Then a brash young Dallas linebacker by the name of Thomas "Hollywood" Henderson tried to open up some of those old wounds in an attempt to get inside Bradshaw's head and bring him back down to earth.

Hearing that Bradshaw did not have the grades to be accepted to Louisiana State University, Henderson commented to the press that Bradshaw couldn't spell "cat" if you spotted him the *c* and the *a*. It was a memorable quip and became the story of the Super Bowl, as all the old Bradshaw stereotypes reared their ugly heads again. Henderson had made the comment hoping it would affect Bradshaw's performance. And indeed it did—but in the opposite way Henderson had intended.

From the onset, it looked like it would be an offensive showcase. Former Heisman Trophy–winning running back Tony Dorsett torched the Pittsburgh defense for 34 yards on the game's opening drive, but a Dallas fumble squandered an early scoring opportunity. The Steelers then cashed in when Bradshaw connected with wideout John Stallworth down the right sideline for a 28-yard touchdown.

But on Pittsburgh's next two series, Bradshaw slumped, tossing an interception and then coughing up a fumble, the latter of which led to the game-tying touchdown on a long Roger Staubach-to-Tony Hill scoring pass to wrap up an eventful first quarter. Bradshaw turned the ball over again on the next series as well, this time fumbling after a crushing hit by Henderson. Mike Hegman scooped up the loose ball and returned it 37 yards for a Dallas touchdown and a 14–7 lead.

It had been a humiliating few minutes for Bradshaw, reminding him of the painful beginning to his NFL career. But he was no longer that young, confused kid. Now he was the league MVP, and, despite the fact that he'd bruised his shoulder on the preceding turnover, on the next series he showed just how good he had become. Once again, he found Stallworth open downfield, this time for a 75-yard touchdown pass to tie the game once more.

The first 20 minutes of this game had been spellbinding—four huge plays for four touchdowns. The teams settled down for the next few minutes with a missed 51-yard field goal by kicker Roy Gerela as the only scoring opportunity. Then, with the Cowboys driving late in the half, Mel Blount picked off a pass at the Steeler 16 with 1:41 left. Rather than sit on the lead and go into the locker room tied, Bradshaw hit Lynn Swann on two consecutive plays that totaled 50 yards. With only 26 seconds remaining and the Steelers facing third and one at the Dallas 7, Bradshaw rolled to his right and lofted a pass that looked like it would sail over everyone in the end zone. But Rocky Bleier leaped higher than anyone would have imagined, catching the pass for a remarkable touchdown—a moment that wound up being the cover of the following week's *Sports Illustrated* and that gave Pittsburgh a 21–14 lead and Bleier a story to regale teammates with for decades to come. "It's like a three-second play," Joe Greene would say years later, "but Rocky can talk about that play for thirty minutes."[1]

The high-scoring first half gave way to a third quarter dominated by defense. Neither team threatened to score until Dallas drove to the Pittsburgh 10 late in the quarter. On third and three, Staubach found veteran tight end Jackie Smith all alone in the end zone. He fired a pass to Smith for the apparent game-tying touchdown, but the ball bounced off Smith's chest and fell incomplete in a play that swung the momentum back to Pittsburgh. Instead of pulling even, the Cowboys settled for a Rafael Septien field goal that made the score 21–17 going into the final quarter.

The final stanza belonged to Bradshaw time. Helped by a controversial 33-yard pass interference call on the Cowboys' Benny Barnes, the Steelers found themselves on the Dallas 17. They were penalized five yards for delay of game, but on the play, Henderson took a cheap shot at Bradshaw, hitting him after the whistle. This incensed the usually mild-mannered Franco Harris, who got in Henderson's face and then demanded the ball in the huddle. He got it and then blasted up the middle for an emphatic touchdown to put the Steelers ahead, 28–17.

The Steelers' grip tightened when Dallas linebacker Randy White fumbled the ensuing kickoff, and young Pittsburgh linebacker Dennis "Dirt" Winston recovered at the Dallas 18. Bradshaw immediately fired a pass to Swann, who made one of his signature leaping grabs in the back of the end zone to give the Steelers a now-commanding 35–17 lead.

With 6:57 left, it appeared Pittsburgh had the game wrapped up. But the Cowboys wouldn't quit, as Staubach engineered an 89-yard touchdown drive to pull them within 11 points with just over two minutes remaining. Dallas then recovered the onside kick and scored again on a Staubach touchdown pass, but just 22 seconds remained and the Cowboys were out of magic. Bleier covered the ensuing kickoff, and Bradshaw knelt down twice to make the Steelers the first team to win three Super Bowl championships.

After a week of being reminded of the sourness of the early part of his career, Bradshaw had delivered the greatest performance of his career with the spotlight shining right in his face. For the first time in his career, he topped 300 yards passing and threw four touchdown passes. And after a week in which he was haunted by three letters—C, A, and T—he finished that Sunday with three other letters attached to his name: M, V, and P.

BOXSCORE

TEAM	1st	2nd	3rd	4th	FINAL
Pittsburgh	7	14	0	14	35
Dallas	7	7	3	14	31

TEAM	PLAY	SCORE
Pittsburgh	Stallworth 28-yard pass from Bradshaw (Gerela kick)	7–0
Dallas	Hill 39-yard pass from Staubach (Septien kick)	7–7
Dallas	Hegman 37-yard fumble return (Septien kick)	7–14
Pittsburgh	Stallworth 75-yard pass from Bradshaw (Gerela kick)	14–14
Pittsburgh	Bleier 7-yard pass from Bradshaw (Gerela kick)	21–14
Dallas	Septien 27-yard field goal	21–17
Pittsburgh	Harris 22-yard run (Gerela kick)	28–17
Pittsburgh	Swann 18-yard pass from Bradshaw (Gerela kick)	35–17
Dallas	Dupree 7-yard pass from Staubach (Septien kick)	35–24
Dallas	Johnson 4-yard pass from Staubach (Septien kick)	35–31

RUSHING

PITT	ATT	YDS	AVE	TD
Harris	20	68	3.4	1
Bleier	2	3	1.5	0
Bradshaw	2	-5	-2.5	0

HOU	ATT	YDS	AVE	TD
Dorsett	16	96	6.0	0
Staubach	4	37	9.3	0
Laidlaw	3	12	4.0	0
Pearson	1	6	6.0	0
Newhouse	8	3	0.4	0

RECEIVING

PITT	REC	YDS	AVE	TD
Swann	7	124	17.7	1
Stallworth	3	115	38.3	2
Grossman	3	29	9.7	0
Bell	2	21	10.5	0
Harris	1	22	2.0	0
Bleier	1	7	7.0	0

DAL	REC	YDS	AVE	TD
Dorsett	5	44	8.8	0
D. Pearson	4	73	18.3	0
Hill	2	49	24.5	1
Johnson	2	30	15.0	1
Dupree	2	17	8.5	1
P. Pearson	2	15	7.5	0

PASSING

PITT	COMP	ATT	PCT	YDS	TD	INT
Bradshaw	17	30	56.7	318	4	1

DAL	COMP	ATT	PCT	YDS	TD	INT
Staubach	17	30	56.7	228	3	1

#2

The Immaculate Reception

Amazing the impact of a single play. In the Steelers' first playoff game in 25 years, it was a single play that defined not only the game but also the beleaguered franchise. A play that not only wiped out 40 years of frustration but that arguably gave them the confidence to begin a dynasty that's still considered one of the greatest in the history of the National Football League.

To say that Franco Harris's spectacular game-winning reception in the first-round 1972 playoff defeat of the Oakland Raiders was anything less than the description above is not giving it the true credit it deserves. After all, it's why the play is always considered among the top moments in NFL history, no matter whose rankings you go by. When you are talking top plays in Steelers history, this discussion begins and ends here.

The '72 Steelers were a story in themselves, the franchise's first truly great team, built with patience and intelligence. They won the AFC Central Division and charged into the playoffs with realistic hopes of reaching the Super Bowl for the first time. In their first postseason contest in a quarter century, they'd host the tough Oakland Raiders, a team that had defeated Pittsburgh on opening day. While their first meeting was an offensive showcase, the playoff at Three Rivers Stadium would be the exact opposite.

In the first half, the Raiders tried to run away from Pittsburgh's dominant defensive lineman Joe Greene on the left side of the Steelers' line. While they were never able to break loose for a long run, they did move the chains and control the clock, even in spite of the ineffective performance of quarterback Daryl Lamonica, who was playing with a bad case of the flu. An early interception by Lamonica gave the Steelers an early scoring opportunity, but kicker Roy Gerela missed a 52-yard field goal to keep the game scoreless.

They would have another opportunity to get on the board in the second quarter but were halted on a fourth-and-one play from the Oakland 31. Noll later regretted the decision not to kick the field goal, particularly when the game remained scoreless at the half, even though the Steelers had controlled much of the first 30 minutes.

In the second half, Bradshaw, who had also been unsuccessful in the first half, changed his strategy. He gave up the long ball, instead hitting shorter passes underneath to Franco Harris. When the Raiders focused on Harris, Bradshaw went back to the bomb-hitting Shanklin with a long pass to set up a short Gerela field goal for the first points of the game. The marginal advantage held up until the fourth quarter.

Following another Lamonica interception, Oakland head coach John Madden replaced him with young Ken Stabler, who was more mobile, yet proved just as ineffective against the tough Steeler defense. Stabler fumbled the ball deep in his own territory midway through the final quarter, and the Steelers cashed in for another field goal to make it 6–0.

Just when all hope appeared gone for the Raiders, Stabler showed a preview of what was to come over the rest of the decade. He took the Raiders to the Pittsburgh 30 and then rolled away from a Steelers' rush and down the field untouched for the go-ahead touchdown with just 1:13 remaining.

The capacity crowd at Three Rivers Stadium was stunned. The only hope was that somehow, after struggling to move the ball all day, Pittsburgh could get in field-goal range. Starting at their own 20, Bradshaw hit Harris for nine yards and then John Fuqua for 11 more. But as the clock ticked down under a minute, Raiders safety Jack Tatum knocked two passes away, and a third attempt fell incomplete. It brought up fourth and 10 with just 22 seconds remaining. Barring a miracle, the Steelers were about to suffer another of the heartbreaking losses that had defined their first 40 years.

Even Art Rooney had given up, hopping on the elevator to go down to the locker room to console his players. As he did, Bradshaw dropped back to pass and immediately came under pressure from the Oakland rush. He desperately fired a pass down the middle of the field for Fuqua, who had broken open momentarily downfield at the Raiders' 34.

But as the ball arrived, Fuqua was leveled by Tatum. The football caromed 11 yards away, where Harris caught it just before it hit the ground. With most of the players unaware what was going on, Franco took off downfield past a stunned Oakland defense and into the end zone. The crowd, just as confused, cheered wildly, knowing that something had happened. But even the officials weren't sure quite what.

The rule at the time stated that if the ball deflected off an offensive player, a second offensive player could not catch it unless it was first touched by a defensive player. The rule was soon changed, making the first touch question irrelevant—but therein lies the controversy of perhaps the most memorable play in football history. The Raiders insisted the ball had hit Fuqua, therefore negating Harris's catch. The Steelers insisted it had bounced of Tatum. Referee Fred Swearington jogged over to the home-team dugout and called his supervisor Art McNally to discuss what he had seen. For a moment, everyone in the stadium held their breath. Then Swearington emerged and raised his arms in the air to signal a touchdown. And with that, hundreds of fans rushed the field.

Five seconds still remained, and, once the field was cleared, the Steelers kicked the extra point and followed that with a harried kickoff before the clock hit zero. It was the franchise's first playoff victory, and it was one no one would forget.

The Raiders were understandably distraught in their locker room. Tatum was indignant. "I didn't touch the ball," he told reporters, "and it touched him [Fuqua]. It's an illegal pass."[1] A tearful George Atkinson added, "We fight for four bleeping quarters and this happens."[2]

Even now, nobody can say for sure exactly what happened on the play, whom the ball hit, and whom it didn't. But in the end, the question is irrelevant. The play itself was like divine intervention, as if a higher being wanted the Steelers to win the game.

As a result of an "Immaculate Reception."

BOXSCORE

TEAM	1st	2nd	3rd	4th	FINAL
Oakland	0	0	0	7	7
Pittsburgh	0	0	3	10	13

TEAM	PLAY	SCORE
Pittsburgh	Gerela 18-yard field goal	0–3
Pittsburgh	Gerela 29-yard field goal	0–6
Oakland	Stabler 30-yard run (Blanda kick)	7–6
Pittsburgh	Harris 60-yard pass from Bradshaw (Gerela kick)	7–13

RUSHING

PITT	ATT	YDS	AVE	TD
Harris	18	64	3.6	0
Fuqua	16	25	1.6	0
Bradshaw	2	19	9.5	0

OAK	ATT	YDS	AVE	TD
Smith	14	57	4.1	0
Hubbard	14	44	3.1	0
Stabler	1	30	30.0	1
Davis	2	7	3.5	0

RECEIVING

PITT	REC	YDS	AVE	TD
Harris	5	96	19.2	1
Shanklin	3	55	18.3	0
Fuqua	1	11	11.0	0
McMakin	1	9	9.0	0
Young	1	4	4.0	0

OAK	REC	YDS	AVE	TD
Chester	3	40	13.3	0
Biletnikoff	3	28	9.3	0
Smith	2	8	4.0	0
Banaszak	1	12	12.0	0
Siani	1	7	7.0	0
Otto	1	5	5.0	0
Hubbard	1	2	2.0	0

PASSING

PITT	COMP	ATT	PCT	YDS	TD	INT
Bradshaw	11	25	44.0	175	1	1

OAK	COMP	ATT	PCT	YDS	TD	INT
Lamonica	6	18	33.3	45	0	2
Stabler	6	12	50.0	57	0	0

STEELERS 27, ARIZONA CARDINALS 23
FEBRUARY 1, 2009

That's How You Be Great

In football, greatness often surfaces in the middle of a lost cause. In the final moments of Super Bowl XLIII, with the Steelers on the brink of a devastating defeat, a player destined for greatness emerged.

With the game on the line, he marched up and down the sidelines, pumping up his teammates and hoping to inspire them. Throughout the second half, he'd continually implored his fellow players. "Let's be great," he shouted. "Let's go down in history now." And as the Steelers took the field with the game on the line, he yelled, "Who dares to be great? I'm daring to be great right now." Whether or not his words inspired his teammates, they inspired him. In the next two minutes, wide receiver Santonio Holmes, a first-round draft pick of the Steelers three years earlier, was about to carve his name in franchise lore.[1]

Holmes had not always been embraced in Pittsburgh. Shortly after he was drafted, he was arrested on Miami Beach for disorderly conduct and then later on a charge of domestic violence.

On the field, he was beginning to show glimpses of why the Steelers had drafted him. He finished 10th in the league with a 16.8 yards-per-reception average his rookie season and was tops in 2007 with a mark of 18.1. He was also becoming one of the best punt returners in the NFL. But in 2008, once again his off-field activities diverted attention from what he did on the gridiron: Holmes had been arrested for marijuana possession. To send a message, head coach Mike Tomlin deactivated him, and the message was received. Holmes stayed out of trouble for the rest of the season and appeared to have turned a corner.

With his life off the field steady, he began to hit his stride on the field. He returned a punt 67 yards for a touchdown in a victory against San Diego in the first round of the playoffs and then snagged a 65-yard scoring toss from Ben Roethlisberger in the AFC Championship a week later.

But Holmes was saving his best for the big show, where the Steelers would face the upstart Arizona Cardinals, who had stunned the NFC to win the conference title despite holding just a 9–7 record. Most thought the game would be a mismatch, and in the early going that's exactly what it looked like.

On the Steelers' first drive, Roethlisberger completed a 38-yard pass to Hines Ward, who hadn't been expected to play after injuring his knee in the AFC title game two weeks before. Ward's catch led to a Pittsburgh field goal, and the Steelers picked up where they left off on their next series, driving 69 yards and surging to a 10–0 lead on a one-yard touchdown plunge by Gary Russell.

Usually when the heavy favorite dominates the underdog early, the game quickly turns into a rout. But veteran Arizona quarterback Kurt Warner had been here before, piloting the St. Louis Rams to a Super Bowl title. Warner sliced through the Pittsburgh secondary on an 83-yard touchdown drive to bring Arizona within three. Then after a Karlos Dansby interception at the Pittsburgh 22 late in the second, the Cardinals reached the 1 with 18 seconds left in the half and a chance to lead a game they looked like they had no chance of winning.

But Pittsburgh linebacker James Harrison fooled Warner into thinking he was expecting a run, instead dropping into coverage and intercepting Warner's pass. Rather than falling to the ground, Harrison embarked on one of the most incredible returns in Super Bowl history. Harrison broke into the open surrounded by his teammates down the right sideline, found more daylight across midfield, and then just as he was caught by Arizona wide receiver Larry Fitzgerald at the Arizona 1, Harrison rolled on top of Fitzgerald and into the end zone before hitting the ground, completing a 100-yard, and giving the Steelers a 17–7 lead.

The Pittsburgh defense remained tough in the third quarter, and a Jeff Reed 21-yard field goal gave the Steelers what appeared to be a comfortable 13-point lead going into the final quarter. And what a quarter it would be.

Warner quickly took Arizona down the field, capping the drive when he connected with Fitzgerald on a fade route in the corner of the end zone to pull the Cardinals within 20–14. After a defensive stop, the Cardinals were unable to put points on the board on their next series but pinned Pittsburgh at its own 1. The Steelers appeared to have things in hand when Holmes caught a 19-yard pass that seemed to give Pittsburgh breathing room and a first down with three minutes left. But offensive lineman Justin Hartwig was penalized for a holding penalty in the end zone on the play, which by rule gave the Cardinals a safety, cutting the margin to 20–16. And perhaps more importantly, they would also get the ball.

On the second play of the ensuing possession, Warner hit Fitzgerald on a slant at the Arizona 43. Fitzgerald bolted past Ike Taylor and took the ball the remaining 57 yards for the go-ahead score with just over two minutes left. After a holding penalty on the first play of the next possession pushed them back to their own 12, the Steelers appeared defeated. Enter Santonio Holmes, first to fire up his teammates and then to deliver for them.

About to be sacked inside his 10, Roethlisberger rolled to his right and found Holmes at the 27 for 14 yards. Then on third down, Roethlisberger stepped up in the pocket to avoid the rush and found Holmes for another 13 yards and a first down at the Pittsburgh 39.

Three plays later from the Arizona 46, Roethlisberger connected with Holmes once again, this time at the Arizona 35. Defensive back Aaron Francisco fell down, and Holmes cruised to the Cardinals' 6 as the Steelers' faithful completed their quick transformation from forlorn to ecstatic. At worst, it appeared the Steelers had a chip-shot field goal to send the game to overtime.

With only 48 seconds left, Roethlisberger thought he had Holmes open in the left corner of the end zone and fired a pass toward him, but the ball went through his hands. On the next play, Roethlisberger threw toward Holmes in the right corner, but this time Holmes was double-covered—and pinned in by the back of the end zone. Somehow, Roethlisberger's pass threaded between a sea of Arizona hands and right into Holmes's. He caught the ball and then more impressively, kept his feet in bounds for a touchdown. A replay review confirmed the call, and the Steelers had taken a 27–23 lead.

On the sideline Holmes screamed to his teammates the same type of message he'd been delivering for the entire game: "That's how you be great!"[2]

Warner still had one last chance and moved his offense to the Pittsburgh 44 with 15 seconds remaining, but LaMarr Woodley sacked him and knocked the ball loose. Pittsburgh's Brett Keisel fell on it, and one of the greatest Super Bowls ever played had reached its conclusion.

The Steelers had their record sixth Super Bowl championship, and Holmes became the third Pittsburgh wide receiver to be named Super Bowl MVP.

He did it with a catch that arguably was the most dramatic not only in the history of the franchise but also in the annals of professional football, one that would be replayed countless times in the years to come.

In that moment, he showed both his teammates and football fans around the world exactly how to be great.

BOXSCORE

TEAM	1st	2nd	3rd	4th	FINAL
Pittsburgh	3	14	3	7	27
Arizona	0	7	0	16	23

TEAM	PLAY	SCORE
Pittsburgh	Reed 18-yard field goal	3–0
Pittsburgh	Russell 1-yard run (Reed kick)	10–0
Arizona	Patrick 1-yard pass from Warner (Rackers kick)	10–7
Pittsburgh	Harrison 100-yard interception return (Reed kick)	17–7
Pittsburgh	Reed 21-yard field goal	20–7
Arizona	Fitzgerald 1-yard pass from Warner (Rackers kick)	20–14
Arizona	Safety, Hartwig penalty holding in end zone	20–16
Arizona	Fitzgerald 64-yard pass from Warner (Rackers kick)	20–23
Pittsburgh	Holmes 6-yard pass from Roethlisberger (Reed kick)	27–23

RUSHING

PITT	ATT	YDS	AVE	TD
Parker	19	53	2.8	0
Moore	1	6	6.0	0
Roethlisberger	3	2	0.7	0
Russell	2	-3	-1.5	1

ARIZ	ATT	YDS	AVE	TD
James	9	33	3.7	0
Warner	1	0	0.0	0
Arrington	1	0	0.0	0
Hightower	1	0	0.0	0

RECEIVING

PITT	REC	YDS	AVE	TD
Holmes	9	131	14.6	1
Miller	5	57	11.4	0
Ward	2	43	21.5	0
Davis	1	6	6.0	0
Spaeth	1	6	6.0	0
Moore	1	4	4.0	0
Parker	1	-2	-2.0	0

ARIZ	REC	YDS	AVE	TD
Boldin	8	84	10.5	0
Fitzgerald	7	127	18.1	2
Breaston	6	71	11.8	0
James	4	28	7.0	0
Arrington	2	35	17.5	0
Hightower	2	13	6.5	0
Urban	1	18	18.0	0
Patrick	1	1	1.0	1

PASSING

PITT	COMP	ATT	PCT	YDS	TD	INT
Roethlisberger	21	30	70.0	256	1	1

ARIZ	COMP	ATT	PCT	YDS	TD	INT
Warner	31	43	72.1	377	3	1

Notes

#50

1. Chester L. Smith, "Mose Kelch's Story Book Kicks Win for Pirates," *Pittsburgh Press,* Sept. 28, 1933.

#49

1. Al Abrams, "Nice Time Had by All," *Pittsburgh Post-Gazette,* Nov. 30, 1970.

#48

1. Vito Stellino, "Hard Way Steelers Now Looking at Colts," *Pittsburgh Post-Gazette,* Dec. 13, 1976.

2. Phil Musick, "A Glorious Resurrection," *Pittsburgh Post-Gazette,* Dec. 13, 1976.

#45

1. Ron Cook, "Chumps?" *Pittsburgh Press,* Dec. 16, 1984.

#43

1. Al Abrams, "Now That All Is Settled," *Pittsburgh Post-Gazette,* Jan. 28, 1969.

#42

1. Phil Musick, "Hard Lesson for America's Team," *Pittsburgh Post-Gazette,* Oct. 29, 1979.

2. Vito Stellino, "Steelers Dominate Bewildered Cowboys," *Pittsburgh Post-Gazette,* Oct. 29, 1979.

#39

1. Tom Williams, "Defense Saves Day for Steelers," *Youngstown Vindicator,* Jan. 4, 1998.

2. Gerald Ezkenazi, "Steelers Lose Gamble but Win Game Anyway," *New York Times,* Jan. 4, 1998.

3. Tom Williams, "Defense Saves Day for Steelers," *Youngstown Vindicator,* Jan. 4, 1998.

#38

1. Ed Bouchette, "Holmes' Score Clinches AFC North for Steelers," *Pittsburgh Post-Gazette,* Dec. 15, 2008.

#36

1. Ed Bouchette, "Wallace Pulls in Winning TD to End Skid," *Pittsburgh Post-Gazette,* Dec. 21, 2009.

2. Ibid.

#35

1. Ed Bouchette, "Steelers' Defense Equals Game-winning Touchdown, Four Turnovers and Three Sacks," *Pittsburgh Post-Gazette,* Dec. 8, 2008.

2. Judy Battista, "On Frozen Day, Steelers Offense Thaws Just Enough," *New York Times,* Dec. 8, 2008.

#33

1. Associated Press, "Steelers Work OT for AFC Central Lead," *Youngstown Vindicator,* Nov. 6, 1995.
2. Ibid.
3. Ibid.

#31

1. NFL Films Game of the Week, NFL Network, Dec. 21, 2005.

#30

1. NFL Films Game of the Week, NFL Network, Jan. 6, 2006.

#29

1. Vito Stellino, "Steelers Trample Colts, 40–14," *Pittsburgh Post-Gazette,* Dec. 20, 1976.
2. Vito Stellino, "With Money on the Line: The Steelers Will Take Terry," *Pittsburgh Post-Gazette,* Dec. 20, 1976.

#28

1. Associated Pres, "Reed's 19th Straight Made Field Goal Gives Pittsburgh Win," www.espn.com, Jan. 15, 2005.

#27

1. Jack Sell, "Steelers Win First Title in 40 Years," *Pittsburgh Post-Gazette,* Dec. 18, 1972.
2. Ibid.

#25

1. Associated Press, "Steelers Snap Patriots' 21-Game Win Streak," www.si.com, Oct. 31, 2004.
2. Ibid.

#24

1. Pat Livingston, "Unconditional Surrender," *Pittsburgh Press,* Jan. 8, 1979.
2. Ibid.

#23

1. Associated Press, "Steelers First to Win Three on Road to Reach Super Bowl Since 1985," www.espn.com, Jan. 22, 2006.

#22

1. Ron Cook, "Block Party," *Pittsburgh Press,* Oct. 15, 1984.
2. Ibid.
3. John Clayton, "Stallworth Became the Hero . . . by His Own Design," *Pittsburgh Press,* Oct. 15, 1984.
4. Ron Cook, "Block Party," *Pittsburgh Press,* Oct. 15, 1984.

#21

1. Ed Bouchette, "Steelers Top Oilers, 26–23," *Pittsburgh Post-Gazette,* Jan. 1, 1990.
2. Ibid.

#20

1. Gerry Dulac, "Comeback Versus Raven among Most Satisfying," *Pittsburgh Post-Gazette,* Jan. 17, 2011.
2. "Steelers Reach AFC Title Game as Ben Roethlisberger, Turnovers Bury Ravens," www.espn.com, Jan. 15, 2011.

#19

1. Mike Bieres, "Did Racism Lift Bradshaw over Gilliam in 1974? An Indiana Writer Says Yes," *Beaver County Times,* Aug. 23, 2011.
2. Ibid.

#18

1. Charley Feeney, "Do-It-All Steeler—John Stallworth," *Pittsburgh Post-Gazette,* Jan. 5, 1976.

#16

1. "Steelers-Jets Preview," www.espn.com, Jan. 23, 2011.

2. Rachel Cohen, "Rex Ryan: Jets Will Play Steelers Trophies Too," *Deseret News,* Jan. 21, 2011.

3. "Steelers Headed to Super Bowl after Jets Come Up Short," www.espn.com, Jan. 23, 2011.

#14

1. John Adams, "Steelers Come Back, Stun Denver," *Pittsburgh Post-Gazette,* Dec. 31, 1984.

#12

1. "Heated Remarks from Hawaii," www.si.com, Feb. 2, 2003.

2. "Steelers Survive as Colts Attempt to Tie Sails Wide," www.espn.com, Jan. 15, 2006.

#11

1. "Maddox Leads the Steelers All the Way Back," www.espn.com, Jan. 5, 2003.

2. Ibid.

#9

1. "Polamalu's INT Return Secures Steelers' Super Bowl Berth," www.espn.com, Jan. 18, 2009.

2. Ibid.

#7

1. David Fink, "Raided Steelers Manhandle Oakland, 24–13," *Pittsburgh Post-Gazette,* Dec. 30, 1974.

2. Vito Stellino "Rooney Wins Like He Loses—With Class All the Way," *Pittsburgh Post-Gazette,* Dec. 30, 1974.

#6

1. Ed Bouchette, "Thumbs Up," *Pittsburgh Post-Gazette,* Jan. 15, 1996.

2. Ibid.

#5

1. "NFL Best—Top 5 Greatest Wide Receivers of All Time," www.hubpages.com.

2. *America's Game-Pittsburgh Steelers: Story of Six Championships.* Disc 2, 1975 season (Mt. Laurel, NJ: NFL Films, 2009), DVD.

#3

1. *America's Game-Pittsburgh Steelers: Story of Six Championships.* Disc 3, 1978 season (Mt. Laurel, NJ: NFL Films, 2009), DVD.

#2

1. Vince Leonard, "The Play: It's Torture to Madden and the Raiders," *Pittsburgh Post-Gazette,* Dec. 25, 1972.

2. Ibid.

#1

1. *Pittsburgh Steelers: The Official Super Bowl XLIII DVD,* Vivendi Entertainment, Feb. 24, 2009.

2. Ibid.